Great Thinkers in Economics Series

Series Editor: **A.P. Thirlwall**, Emeritus Professor of Applied Economics, University of Kent, UK.

Great Thinkers in Economics is designed to illuminate the economics of some of the great historical and contemporary economists by exploring the interactions between their lives and work, and the events surrounding them. The books will be brief and written in a style that makes them not only of interest to professional economists, but also intelligible for students of economics and the interested lay person.

Titles include:

William J. Barber
GUNNAR MYRDAL

Paul Davidson
JOHN MAYNARD KEYNES

Peter D. Groenewegen
ALFRED MARSHALL

Forthcoming titles include:

Esben Sloth Andersen
JOSEPH A. SCHUMPETER

Michael Szenberg and Lal Ramrattan
FRANCO MODIGLIANI

Charles Rowley
JAMES McGILL BUCHANAN

Michael A. Lebowitz
KARL MARX

John King
NICOLAS KALDOR

Alessandro Roncaglia
PIERO SRAFFA

Julio Lopez and Michaël Samuel Assous
KALECKI'S THEORY OF CAPITALIST ECONOMIES

Gerhard Michael Ambrosi
ARTHUR C. PIGOU

J. R. Stanfield
JOHN KENNETH GALBRAITH

Warren Young Esteban Perez
ROY HARROD

G. C. Harcourt and Prue Kerr
JOAN ROBINSON AND HER CIRCLE

Roger Middleton
ROBERT SOLOW

Gavin Kennedy
ADAM SMITH

Gordon Fletcher
SIR DENNIS HOLME ROBERTSON

Great Thinkers in Economics
Series Standing Order ISBN 978–1–4039–8555–2 (Hardback)
978–1–4039–8556–9 (Paperback)
(outside North America only)

You can receive future titles in this series as they are published by placing a standing order. Please contact your bookseller or, in case of difficulty, write to us at the address below with your name and address, the title of the series and the ISBN quoted above.

Customer Services Department, Macmillan Distribution Ltd, Houndmills, Basingstoke, Hampshire RG21 6XS, England

Gunnar Myrdal

An Intellectual Biography

William J. Barber

palgrave
macmillan

First published 2008 by
PALGRAVE MACMILLAN
Houndmills, Basingstoke, Hampshire RG21 6XS and
175 Fifth Avenue, New York, N.Y. 10010
Companies and representatives throughout the world

PALGRAVE MACMILLAN is the global academic imprint of the Palgrave Macmillan division of St. Martin's Press, LLC and of Palgrave Macmillan Ltd. Macmillan® is a registered trademark in the United States, United Kingdom and other countries. Palgrave is a registered trademark in the European Union and other countries.

ISBN 978-1-349-54785-2 ISBN 978-0-230-28901-7 (eBook)
DOI 10.1057/9780230289017

A catalogue record for this book is available from the British Library.

A catalog record for this book is available from the Library of Congress.

Transferred to Digital Printing in 2014

To Paul Streeten: Inspiring Teacher, Distinguished Scholar, and Valued Friend

Contents

Preface

This is an intellectual biography of one of the most creative and influential economic thinkers of the twentieth century. As such, it is focused on Myrdal's ideas – how they were shaped, how they evolved over time, and how they had impact – rather than on the details of his personal life. A full-scale conventional biography of Gunnar Myrdal has yet to be written. But much of that gap has been filled by two excellent books: Sissela Bok, *Alva Myrdal: A Daughter's Memoir* and Walter A. Jackson, *Gunnar Myrdal and America's Conscience: Social Engineering and Racial Liberalism*, 1938–1987.

I am also grateful to Sissela Bok for her careful reading of the manuscript and for sharing insights into her father's thinking. Darwin H. Stapleton, the Executive Director of the Rockefeller Archive Center, has kindly permitted me to cite materials in their collection. I also wish to record my gratitude to the Department of Culture in the City of Stockholm for granting permission to use extracts from ASIAN DRAMA: AN INQUIRY INTO THE POVERTY OF NATIONS.

I acknowledge with thanks the help of Anna Ankar Barron, both for her translations of documents from the Swedish and for her skill in preparing the typescript. I am also grateful to the Trustees of Wesleyan University for a project grant that covered part of the expenses incurred in readying the study for the press.

In the interest of full disclosure, I should report that I came to know Gunnar Myrdal personally as a member of the research team that worked on the South Asian development study, entitled *Asian Drama: An Inquiry Into the Poverty of Nations*, published in three volumes in 1968.

My greatest debt is to Paul Streeten, a colleague and friend of long standing, whose critical eye has improved my drafts. To him, this book is respectfully dedicated.

W. J. B.

Prologue

The credentials of Gunnar Myrdal (1898–1987) for inclusion in the select company of Great Thinkers in Economics are impressive. His career was noteworthy for the originality and penetration of his insights. Other qualities were no less striking – in particular, the range, depth, and breadth of his scholarship.

As a young member of what was to become known as 'the Stockholm School,' he first made a mark for his contributions to economic theory in the late 1920s and early 1930s. His doctoral dissertation (which has been published only in Swedish) was an exercise in pure micro-economic theory in which he studied the way in which prices, profits, and capital values were influenced by anticipations of future changes in the market environment. Soon thereafter, he turned attention to problems in macro-economic theory, with special reference to the stability (or otherwise) in monetary conditions. (His work in this vein appeared in Swedish in 1931 and in German in 1933; an English version was delayed until 1939, when it appeared as *Monetary Equilibrium*.) The role of anticipated future conditions again was central to the argument, as reflected in the distinctions he drew between intended and actual saving and investment (which, with an assist from his translator, became *ex ante* and *ex post* in the German edition of 1933). These conceptions – which form the analytic core of Keynes's *General Theory of Employment, Interest and Money*, published in 1936 – were originated by Myrdal. If his contribution had been available to readers of English before 1936, it is interesting to speculate whether the 'revolution' in macroeconomic theory of the depression decade would be referred to as 'Myrdalian' as much as 'Keynesian.'

The first phase of his career included a critique of the tendency of mainstream economic theory to incorporate implicit value judgments into its conceptual framework. And these contained political biases. Myrdal demonstrated that the claims of value-neutral innocence made for economic theory were erroneous. Accordingly, economic theorists who maintained that their work was 'scientific' should be viewed skeptically. This study appeared in Swedish in

1930 and in German in 1932. An English translation – entitled *The Political Element in the Development of Economic Theory* – was published in 1953 and continues to be widely read. In all of his mature work, a preoccupation with the exposure of biases can be observed.

Myrdal's career entered a second phase – this time as a political economist – when he began to focus on the implications of his macroeconomic theorizing for the conduct of fiscal and monetary policies. As a consultant to the Swedish Minister of Finance, he produced a lengthy memorandum on depression-fighting policies in 1932. In 1936, he was elected to the upper house of the Swedish parliament as a member of the Social Democratic Party. In company with his wife – Alva Myrdal – he produced a major study in the mid-1930s analyzing the economic consequences of declining population growth. This, in turn, led the two of them to formulate a major program to reverse Sweden's population decline. What this amounted to was a policy blueprint of the Swedish welfare state.

Myrdal returned to full-time scholarly research in 1938, when he was invited by an American foundation to direct a study of the Negro problem in the United States. His approach to this issue was organized around a novel analytic construct: a tension between ideals and realities. The ideal – as presented in what he described as the 'American creed' – called for a society with equal rights and equal opportunities for all. This was embodied in the official rhetoric of the Declaration of Independence and the Constitution. The reality of American race relations in the 1930s stood in sharp contrast. In this mismatch, he argued, ideas could be a force to promote positive change. This scholarly strategy was clearly in harmony with his analysis of the way expectations could have an impact on price formation and on decisions to save and to invest. In this instance, he was painting with a much broader brush – one built around a multi-disciplinary approach that transcended the arbitrarily drawn boundary lines between economic, political, sociological, anthropological, or historical analysis. This massive research project appeared in 1944 under the title *An American Dilemma: The Negro Problem and Modern Democracy*. Here his own ideas had impact on the course of history. The argument of *An American Dilemma* provided much of the intellectual buttress to the decision of the US Supreme Court to declare racial segregation in public facilities to be un-Constitutional.

Between 1943 and 1947, Myrdal was engaged in public activities that utilized his professional skills. He resumed the seat in the Swedish parliament that he had vacated when leaving for the United States to study the Negro problem there. For 2 years (1945–1947) he served in the Swedish cabinet as Minister of Commerce. In the next decade (1947–1957) he was the founding head of a newly created United Nations Organization, the Economic Commission for Europe (ECE), headquartered in Geneva, Switzerland. Under his leadership, this organization produced fundamental studies into the post-war condition of Europe's economies to inform decision-makers on policy-making by the respective governments. The ECE decade also re-engaged him with problems in the international economy. Scholarly work that challenged the premises of conventional international trade theory followed.

When leaving the post of Executive Secretary of the Economic Commission for Europe, Myrdal embarked upon another major scholarly project that was to consume him for the next 10 years. This was an investigation of the development problems of the newly independent countries of South Asia. He had developed an enthusiasm for an institutional approach to economics in his work on the Negro problem in America. This enthusiasm was extended and reinforced in the new study *Asian Drama: An Inquiry into the Poverty of Nations* (1968). This work, which appeared in three volumes (including sixteen appendices), was a frontal assault on the thinking then conventional about the economic growth prospects in underdeveloped countries. Myrdal's originality – and his willingness to attack received wisdom – was again on display.

Throughout his career, Gunnar Myrdal was an innovator who supplied rich analytic insights ahead of most others. Not least, he was willing to extend the scope of his inquiries in ways that cut across disciplines and continents.

1
Beginnings and Early Intellectual Influences

Gunnar Myrdal was born in 1898 in the Swedish province of Dalarna. His origins were humble: he could trace three centuries of peasant stock in his ancestry. His father, however, departed from that occupational pattern. Though equipped with little formal education, he succeeded as a largely self-taught member of the building trade, specializing in the construction of railway stations. His mother, who also had slight exposure to formal education, was a conscientious Lutheran. The young Myrdal and his three younger siblings were instructed in the teachings of that tradition – as were their contemporaries who participated in the 'Kristendom' (Christianity) program then obligatory in Swedish schools. As an adult, Myrdal lapsed from churchgoing. Even so, Biblical overtones lived on in his intellectual style.

When Myrdal was 6 years old, the family settled in Stockholm. Despite this shift in residence, the family continued to identify with its roots in the province of Dalarna. Situated some 250 kilometers to the northwest of the nation's capital, Dalarna occupied an honored place in Swedish history. Its rough terrain had served its inhabitants well when called upon to defend their own – and the nation's – independence. In the sixteenth century, Dalarna had withstood the Danish invasions and had supplied the wherewithal that enabled Gustavus Vasa to rally Swedish forces to liberate the country. The province's citizens cherished their reputation for steadfastness in character and for their determined independence. Throughout his life, Myrdal spoke proudly about his links with that tradition.

Myrdal spent his adolescent years in one of the better public high schools (the Norra Real) in Stockholm. In 1918, he enrolled in the University of Stockholm to study law. An acquaintance made in the summer of 1919 was to have a career-reorienting impact. He then met Alva Reimer, an attractive young woman 3 years his junior. Educationally ambitious and possessed with a lively intellectual curiosity, she felt stifled in a family that offered little support for her aspirations. Her father, though a social democrat by conviction, did not fully appreciate her strengths, and her mother, who led the life of a recluse, was emphatically unsympathetic. Such attitudes were not all that unusual in the Sweden of that time: conventions of the day held that most women should confine themselves to household duties and that exposure to higher education – with a few exceptions – should be the exclusive province of men.

The collaboration between Gunnar Myrdal and Alva Reimer (who became Mrs Myrdal in 1924) was to be highly productive over the years. For Alva, the Gunnar connection was intellectually liberating and a catalytic agent in her successful quest to complete a degree in psychology. For Gunnar, the Alva connection – with her background in the Social Democratic youth movement – energized his consciousness with regard to society's imperfections.

In 1923, Gunnar completed a degree in law from the University of Stockholm. This event coincided with a realization that a legal career was not to his taste. The life of a lawyer, he then concluded, would fail to satisfy his desire to understand how societies really functioned. At Alva's urging he decided to take up advanced studies in economics. As he later wrote,

> I passed my LL.B. . . . in a relatively short time already in the spring of 1923. But I was, then, intellectually quite completely crushed and deeply depressed. It was Alva who saved me. She suggested that I should devote myself to a study of political economy which was more like the natural sciences and mathematics. She purchased Gustav Cassel's *Theoretische Sozialökonomie*. I found parts of it somewhat incomprehensible, but realize now, when I leaf through the old copy, that my old queries were fairly correctly placed. I then took it upon myself to read through all that was printed in the *Economisk tidskrift* from the first volume in 1899.[1]

The state of Swedish economics in the mid-1920s

For anyone embarking on professional studies in economics in the 1920s, Stockholm was a very good address. The country was small – Sweden's population at that time was approximately six million – but it contained a constellation of stars in the discipline. On a *per capita* basis, no other country could match Sweden's production of economists of international stature.

In the eyes of contemporaries, the most prominent among them was Gustav Cassel (1866–1944), the occupant of the major chair at the University of Stockholm from 1904 to 1933. Indeed, he was reckoned to be the foremost economist in the world in the 1920s. In Schumpeter's assessment, Cassel was 'the most influential leader of our science in the 1920s – for such he was, whatever his critics (including myself) may say.'[2] His reputation was built on his analysis of the international monetary situation, post-World War I, in which he was an uncompromising advocate of restoration of the gold standard. In addition, his theoretical discussion of the conditions required in a uniformly progressing state – in which he maintained that the rate of growth in income should equal the rate of growth in the stock of capital – has been credited with anticipating by at least a decade and a half a central insight that would later be identified with the Harrod–Domar growth model.[3]

Cassel's textbook – *The Theory of Social Economy* – went through multiple editions in various translations and enjoyed a multinational audience. He was a conspicuous, as well as a frequent, commentator on economic issues in the popular press. As a teacher and lecturer, he was a force who won the acclaim of his students, including those who did not share his conservative political perspective. He and Myrdal were to form a close bond, even though they certainly did not see eye-to-eye politically. In an obituary notice, Myrdal spoke warmly about Cassel's ability to inspire students and colleagues and about his dedication to the highest standards of scholarhip.[4] Myrdal also respected Cassel for 'a healthy realism in his approch to economic problems, a desire to avoid metaphysical speculation and to get down to facts and figures.'[5]

An aspect of Cassel's international impact can be observed in the roster of economists who contributed to a Festschrift marking his retirement from his chair at the University of Stockholm. Altogether,

14 nations were represented: Sweden, Norway, Denmark, Finland, Switzerland, Belgium, Germany, Hungary, Italy, France, the United Kingdom, Czechoslovakia, the Netherlands, and the United States. In addition, there were two submissions from economists in the employ of the League of Nations Secretariat. Not surprisingly, all the members of Sweden's first team of economists (including Myrdal) contributed. More striking is the fact that the United States supplied more contributors – 12 in all – than any other country. The list was impressive: James Angell (Columbia), J. M. Clark (Columbia), John R. Commons (Wisconsin), Paul Douglas (Chicago), Frank Graham (Princeton), Alvin Hansen (Minnesota), Jacob Hollander (Johns Hopkins), Edwin W. Kemmerer (Princeton), Frank Knight (Chicago), Ernest M. Patterson (Pennsylvania), E. R. A. Seligman (Columbia), and Carl Snyder (New York Federal Reserve Bank).[6]

Cassel's prestige notwithstanding, his economics had its idiosyncrasies. For example, he rejected the marginal utility approach to the theory of demand, a position for which he was roundly criticized. (Myrdal, it should be noted, faithfully absorbed this bit of Cassel's doctrine.) Cassel's insistence on purchasing power parity as the explanation of foreign exchange rates was also a target of criticism.

Another formidable figure was Knut Wicksell (1851–1926). Unfortunately, his creativity was better appreciated posthumously than it was during his lifetime. He was among the pioneers in the formulation of the marginal productivity theory of income distribution. The achievements for which he is best known are associated with his account of aggregative economic instability. The root of this problem, he maintained, could be traced to divergences between the market rate of interest and the natural rate of interest (defined as the rate that would equilibrate the flow of savings with the sums sought by investors in capital goods). When the market rate fell below the natural rate, capital spending would generate inflationary pressures; conversely, if the market rate exceeded the natural rate, the economy would be subject to deflationary pressures. Price level stability could be achieved only when the two rates converged. Wicksell's teaching also had a further message. Departures from equilibrium could not be expected to be self-correcting. On the contrary, they might well breed further departures from the initial position. This conclusion reflected Wicksell's conception of cumulative causation in which an initial disturbance would have an inherent tendency to magnify itself. After his death, these features of his analysis gained increased resonance with the crisis of the Great Depression. (The younger generation of Swedish economists, including Myrdal, who came into professional maturity in the late 1920s and early 1930s regarded themselves as neo-Wicksellians and were to be known as members of the 'Stockholm School.')

It is sad to report that Wicksell's contemporaries did not come to terms with his analytic originality. This failing can largely be attributed to the fact that their vision was obstructed by Wicksell's unconventional lifestyle (which contained much to disturb bourgeois sensibilities). He preached neo-Malthusianism and spoke openly about the importance of insuring easy access to contraceptives. But that was not all. He had a common law marriage; he refused to swear an oath of allegiance to the King; and he argued that Swedish defense against, say, an invasion from Russia would be futile and that it would be best to scrap the military establishment. Rather late in life, Wicksell managed in 1901 to secure a professorial post at the University of Lund, which he held until retirement in 1917. He then moved to Stockholm, where he remained professionally active as a member of the Economics Club, as a sometime consultant to government, and as an informal adviser to graduate students. Wicksell's influence was very much a part of the economics culture that Myrdal knew as a graduate student, but there is no evidence of personal acquaintance between the two.[7]

Little known outside Sweden, but a force within it, was David Davidson (1854–1942). He occupied a chair at the University of Uppsala from 1889 until his retirement in 1919. His commentaries on monetary issues were admired by contemporaries, but they appeared only in Swedish (as was the case with all of his writings). He made a fundamental contribution as the founding proprietor and editor of Sweden's first economic journal, *Ekonomisk tidskrift*, which appeared in 1899. (This journal was rechristened in 1965 as *The Swedish Journal of Economics* and was published in English. In 1975, it was transformed once more as *The Scandinavian Journal of Economics*.) Davidson's initiative – in which a journal was used as the primary vehicle for professional communication – was clearly in keeping with advanced practice in other countries.[8]

One of the younger members of the constellation, Eli Heckscher (1879–1952), a chair-holder in the University of Stockholm, specialized in economic history. He was also an able economic theorist: an article he published in 1919 formed the basis for what later became known as the Heckscher–Ohlin theorem positing that countries tend to export commodities produced through intensive use of the home factors available in relative abundance. Throughout his career, he resolutely called for greater attention to theory in the writing of economic history. Though he produced highly regarded histories of Sweden, the work for which he is best known internationally is a classic study of *Mercantilism*, which appeared in an English translation in 1935.

Gösta Bagge (1882–1951), the youngest member of the group, was appointed to a chair in the University of Stockholm in 1921 that was designed to promote specialist studies in social policy. He was conservative by instinct and later became the head of the Conservative Party. His interaction with other economists in the early 1920s was restricted because of his discomfort in the company of Wicksellian radicalism. Nevertheless, he proved to be a stalwart in procuring funding from the Rockefeller Foundation in New York to finance ambitious historical studies of national income, wages, and the cost of living in Sweden. Myrdal was later to participate in a part of this enterprise.

Though their specialisms were different, each of these figures spoke with a distinctive voice. Most, however, shared a common political persuasion. Cassel, Davidson, and Bagge took a conservative line and were generally suspicious of government intervention in the economy. Heckscher was similarly disposed: after all, his study of mercantilism had been a sermon denouncing the wrong-headedness of government attempts to manage the economy. Wicksell was the outlier. He stood for social democracy and endorsed experimentation with socialist initiatives. Wicksell took particular pains to distance himself from Cassel. In 1919, he published a devastating review of Cassel's *Theory of Social Economy* in the *Ekonomisk tidskrift*. Cassel was faulted on substantive issues – for example, his rejection of marginal utility was sharply attacked. Wicksell was further disturbed by a more general shortcoming in the work, namely Cassel's propensity to claim ideas as original that had, in fact, been appropriated from others. For example, he wrote that 'Cassel's indebtedness to [Walras] is obviously very great, but instead of showing the gratitude he ought to have expressed, he does not mention Walras' name once in the whole book.'[9] Thereafter, Cassel and Wicksell were not on speaking terms.

These differences notwithstanding, the Swedish stars of the 1920s shared some fundamental presuppositions. They all believed that the discipline of economics should be of service to the common good. And they also believed that professional economists had a responsibility to inform public opinion. To that end, they all contributed to public debate by publishing in the popular press.

Altogether, graduate students at the University of Stockholm in the mid-1920s had a wealth of resources to draw upon. But they did not rely solely on the stimulus that the professoriate could provide. There was a pool of talent within their own ranks and it would reach maturity in the early 1930s when a second generation of stars identified themselves as members of the 'Stockholm School.' In addition to Myrdal, this group included Erik Lindahl, Bertil Ohlin, Erik Lundberg, and Dag Hammarskjöld.

Graduate studies in economics

In 1924, Myrdal embarked on a doctoral degree program at the University of Stockholm with Cassel as his mentor. Myrdal expressed a desire to investigate the dynamics of pricing, a proposal that Cassel warmed to. In his own work, Cassel had elaborated the Walrasian version of neo-classical price theory (even if the stimulus from Walras remained unacknowledged). The achievement here was a demonstration that equilibrium prices could be established simultaneously throughout the economy, subject to certain restrictive conditions. But this – as Cassel recognized – was by no means the end of the story: the method employed was essentially static. Cassel's formulation proceeded from the premise that three determinants of prices were given: tastes of buyers that shaped the character of demand; the technical conditions of production; and the quantities available of the factors of production.[10] Over time, these preconditions might well be subject to changes arising from exogenous forces, and the path toward a new equilibrium could then be examined. But the nature of the initiating change itself was not within the purview of this analytical setup.

As Myrdal acknowledged, his doctoral dissertation – entitled *Prisbildningsproblemet och föränderligheten* (*The Problem of Price Formation and Changeability*) – was structured within a Casselian framework. He later recalled, 'My first major theoretical work on the integration of anticipations into the theory of price formation owes much to Cassel, and more in regard to general approach than to details.'[11] But he quickly moved beyond Cassel by arguing that a fourth primary determinant of prices should be incorporated into the analysis, namely expectations about the future course of prices. Such anticipations could be expected to play a crucial role in the behavior of buyers and sellers. According to Myrdal, 'changes whether they are completely foreseen or not exert their effects on the economic process long before they actually take place' because 'price formation takes place in human minds.'[12] Different states of expectation could be imagined, each with differing effects on equilibrium prices. But, in each instance, the dynamic outcome would differ from that reached under static conditions. This was the core issue in Myrdal's conception of dynamic theory.

There was innovation in this procedure, but it should be noted that it was embedded in a neo-classical tradition that Myrdal was later to reject forcefully. At this early stage in his career, he was obviously comfortable with – and proficient at – abstract model-building. Inherent in this intellectual style was hostility toward the institutionalist approach to the discipline with its suspicions about the usefulness of abstract theorizing. Indeed, from that perspective, what Myrdal projected as 'dynamic' in 1927 was hardly 'dynamic' at all. A truly dynamic approach would require – as an institutionalist like Thorstein Veblen would maintain – that the analyst should properly focus on explaining what caused changes in tastes and techniques. That line of argument was then alien to Myrdal's way of thinking. He would later reverse himself on the relevance of an institutionalist perspective. Late in life, he expressed doubts about his capacity at that stage to comprehend the theoretical arguments he had deployed in *The Problem of Price Formation and Changeability*.[13]

Myrdal's dissertation won him a doctoral degree with the highest possible honors. This gave him the credential necessary to pursue an academic career. This study has not been translated from the Swedish, despite Cassel's urgings. Concerning the absence of an English translation of the dissertation, Cassel wrote as follows in December 1929 (when both Myrdals were in the United States as recipients of fellowships funded by the Rockefeller Foundation):

> You say that you are tired of your theoretical studies and you look upon the English translation as a task which is too trying. . . . But do not think that you can leave the great problem of changeability, which you have now made a first attempt to put in its proper perspective within the economic theory. . . . I have tried to widen the static viewpoint and to extract from it as much as possible. I also believe that the foundation I have given to this field must last and form the starting point in elementary teaching. . . . The foundation of the dynamic economy is your task and some day you have to reach such a clarity in this matter, that you can give the world an elementary and fully understandable guidance to the dynamics of the economy. This is after all the categorical imperative, which life has put in front of you.[14]

The lack of an English or German translation meant that the work had little impact beyond Sweden. A complimentary notice by Myrdal's friend, Erik Lindahl, did appear in the *Economic Journal* (the organ of Britain's Royal Economic Society) in 1929. Lindahl described it as 'an advance in the right direction.'[15]

Though *The Problem of Price Formation and Changeability* was cast in a mold that Myrdal later abandoned, it did introduce two themes that persisted in his later work. Emphasis on the impact of expectations on economic performance foreshadowed the *ex ante* and *ex post* conceptions of saving and investment developed in *Monetary Equilibrium* in its second version in 1933. The attention to mental states more generally is congruent with aspects of the argumentation in *An American Dilemma: The Negro Problem and Modern Democracy*, 1944.

Notes

1. G. Myrdal, as quoted by Kumaraswamy Velupillai, 'Reflections on Gunnar Myrdal's Contributions to Economic Theory,' *Gunnar Myrdal and His Works*, Gilles Dostaler, Dianne Ethier, and Laurent Lepage, eds (Montreal: Harvest House, 1992), pp. 133–34.
2. J. A. Schumpeter, *History of Economic Analysis* (Oxford University Press, 1954), p. 1154.
3. An English translation of Cassel's text on this point is reproduced by P. Streeten, the author of Appendix 3, Volume 3 of *Asian Drama: An Inquiry into the Poverty of Nations* (New York: Twentieth Century Fund, 1968), pp. 1969–70.

4. G. Myrdal, 'Gustav Cassel in Memoriam (1866–1944),' English translation by G. Ohlin, *Oxford Institute of Economics and Statistics Bulletin*, 25 (February 1963), 1–10. This obituary originally appeared in Swedish in *Ekonomisk revy*, February 1945.
5. G. Myrdal, *Value in Social Theory* (London: Routledge and Kegan Paul, 1958), p. 242.
6. See *Economic Essays in Honour of Gustav Cassel* (London: George Allen and Unwin, 1933).
7. Wicksell's colorful career is marvelously captured in the biography written by T. Gårdlund. See Gårdlund, *The Life of Knut Wicksell* (Stockholm: Almquist and Wiksell, 1958).
8. Launching of professional journals in economics was very much in vogue in the later nineteenth century. In Britain, the Royal Economic Society produced the *Economic Journal*, starting in 1890. In the United States, the first wave of journals was associated with universities eager to promote newly established graduate programs: for example, *The Quarterly Journal of Economics* (Harvard, 1885); *The Political Science Quarterly* (Columbia, 1886); *The Journal of Political Economy* (University of Chicago, 1892). The American Economic Association was founded in 1885, but did not establish its own journal – *The American Economic Review* – until 1910.
9. K. Wicksell, 'Professor Cassel's System of Economics,' reprinted in his *Lectures on Political Economy*, Volume 1, p. 225. This review has been reproduced in *Swedish Economics* 2, B. Sandelin, ed. (London: Routledge, 1998).
10. G. Cassel, *The Theory of Social Economy*, 1923, p. 152, as reported by B. A. Hansson, *The Stockholm School and the Development of Dynamic Method* (London: Croom Helm, 1982), p. 30.
11. G. Myrdal, *Value in Social Theory*, p. 242.
12. As quoted by B. A. Hansson, op. cit., p. 33.
13. As reported by P. Streeten.
14. Cassel to Myrdal, 9 December 1929, as quoted by B. A. Hansson, op. cit., p. 32.
15. Erik Lindahl, Review of '*Dynamic Pricing*' by G. Myrdal, *Economic Journal*, 39 (March 1929) 89–91.

2

Early Challenges to Orthodoxy: The Political Element in the Development of Economic Theory (first published in 1930)*

Myrdal defended his doctoral dissertation in the Spring of 1927 and received a 'Laudatur' – the highest possible grade, rarely awarded – for his performance. This achievement automatically qualified him for an appointment as a docent (associate professor) in the University. He embraced his new duties with enthusiasm and eagerly sought to make a mark in the profession. He later described his situation at that time as complicated by the fact that his senior colleagues represented 'a hard crust of ability and authority, both tempting and deterring to anybody trying to sprout into independent thinking.'[1]

In public, Myrdal first declared his intellectual independence in January 1928 at Stockholm's Political Economy Club when he charged that the elders had failed to distinguish adequately between 'facts' and 'values' in their theorizing on such matters as 'maximum social welfare' and 'national income.' Professor Eli Heckscher (who was present on this occasion) was reportedly outraged by Myrdal's iconoclasm. Thereafter, personal relations between the two men were strained.[2]

Myrdal developed these themes further in a series of lectures delivered at the University in April–May 1928 under the title 'The Concepts of "Value" and "Utility" in Economic Theory.' In the prospectus presented to the University's registrar he indicated that the course was intended as a 'confrontation with some, in [his] opinion, pretty atavistic ideas in economic theory' and as a critique of 'older economists who are still caught in metaphysical cobwebs.'[3]

Myrdal wrestled with these methodological issues for some 2 years during which he produced the manuscript for the volume entitled

The Political Element in the Development of Economic Theory. The writing in its final stages was done in the United States, where both he and Alva were visiting as recipients of Rockefeller Foundation Fellowships during the academic year 1929–1930. (Simultaneous awards to a husband and wife were unusual: Gunnar had stipulated that he would not accept unless a Fellowship was made available to Alva.) In his application, Gunnar wrote that he planned to study 'American methodology in Economics and the Social Sciences in the U.S.A. and London, England.' Alva's project focused on the methodology of social psychology in the United States. They spent the first portion of their Fellowship period in London, working primarily in The British Museum. The two Myrdals disembarked in New York in mid-October 1929.[4]

From the beginning of Myrdal's work on *The Political Element in the Development of Economic Theory*, it was clear that its focus would be primarily negative. After all, it was inspired by 'the need to protest against the intellectual domination of the older generation.' One of Myrdal's friends – an economist at the University of Copenhagen – referred to the exercise, in jest, as 'parricide.'[5]

The core argument

The Political Element in the Development of Economic Theory was constructed around a close reading of the central texts of classical and neo-classical economics, with particular attention to writers in the British tradition. Along the way, there were some side-glances to the work of American and Swedish economists. Consideration of the German Historical School and Marxism was omitted on grounds that the intellectual barrenness of those doctrines had already been demonstrated.

Throughout the study, one theme predominated, namely the systematic confusion perpetrated by mainstream economics with regard to positive statements – that is, those that could be empirically validated – and normative ones that reflected judgments about what was 'good,' 'desirable,' or 'optimal.' The bulk of the practitioners of political economy, he maintained, were guilty of philosophical error because of their propensity to tolerate elisions between the descriptive analysis of what 'is' and evaluative opinions of what 'ought to be.'

The standard claims of value neutrality in their work were thus very much suspect.

In the first instance, this phenomenon could be observed in the standard terminology deployed by economic theorists. Consider, for example, the following: 'equilibrium,' 'balance,' 'adjustment.' Each can be understood as characterizing a particular (though hypothetical) state of affairs. At the same time, each carried an overtone of a favorable outcome that is 'good' or 'desirable.' Similarly, the use of the term 'function' which appeared to be innocent was, in fact, not so. On this point, Myrdal observed,

> It may, for instance, be said that it is the 'function of the entrepreneur to shoulder the risks' or 'to combine the factors of production' or 'to direct production.'... But in economics it is, as we know, so fatally easy to proceed as follows: 'As a reward for performing this function, he receives a profit,' and thereafter to go further and to regard the fact that the entrepreneur fulfills a 'function' as constituting some kind of justification for the profit he receives.[6]

This difficulty was intensified by the number of concepts in the workaday vocabulary of economists that were directly normative in content: that is, 'utility,' 'value' (when referring to something other than that observable in market exchange), 'welfare,' 'subjective costs.' There was a non-measurable metaphysical dimension in each of those terms. For Myrdal, the metaphysical needed to be purged if economics were to sustain any claims to scientific objectivity. On this matter, his thinking reflected the influence of Axel Hägerström, a Swedish philosopher at the University of Uppsala, whose views were in tune with those of the emerging school of logical positivism in Britain.

How did the discipline of political economy happen to take this shape? Myrdal's answer was that its condition arose initially from the influence of natural law reasoning on the thinking of its founding innovators and, latterly, from the influence of utilitarian doctrines. In the first generation of economic thinkers, a tendency to meld the 'is' and the 'ought' was inherent in their mental processes. Both the Physiocrats and the early classical economists in the British tradition juxtaposed the 'natural' with the 'actual' and concluded that the 'natural price,' the 'natural wage,' and so on were synonymous with a situation that was, by definition, 'good.' Political economists of these persuasions saw nothing improper about this procedure. It was central to their program to contrast the artificial and the man-made economic outcomes (in which a visible hand was heavy) with a non-observable 'natural' state that was easy to idealize. A bias in favor of a regime of *laissez-faire* – which substituted an 'invisible hand' for visible ones – was imbedded in this perspective.

In the nineteenth century, the advent of Benthamite utilitarianism introduced a new terminology, but perpetuated the confusion between the 'is' and the 'ought'. Indeed, the hard-core version of this doctrine proclaimed unashamedly that it had formulated a science of ethics. Its 'maximum happiness' principle defined the objective of human activity. Using the 'felicific calculus,' measures that could be shown to enlarge the net sum of happiness, self-evidently, should be pursued. And it was only a short step beyond this to conclude – as most of those in the mainstream did – that a regime of perfect competition would offer the best prospect for the realization of this objective.

Later in the nineteenth century, the original utilitarian thrust mutated into marginalism. But the fact-value difficulty did not go away. John Bates Clark (1847–1938), the American who pioneered in the formulation of marginal productivity theory, made a convenient target for Myrdal's criticism. Clark was much concerned about the 'ethics of distribution' – indeed his first (and pre-marginal productivity theory) book carried that title. Once his new analytical tool had been contrived, he was convinced that he had found the 'right' answer. If workers – and the other factors of production as well – were remunerated in accordance with the value of their marginal product, then 'distributive justice' would be achieved. Formally, this could be accomplished if conditions of perfect competition prevailed in both product and factor markets.

Over time, criticisms within the British community of economists posed some threats to the utilitarian supremacy. John Stuart Mill, for example, questioned whether or not all forms of pleasure were commensurable. He personally believed that the 'higher' intellectual pleasures were decidedly superior to the 'lower' materialistic and animal pleasures. In addition, doubts were raised about the legitimacy and realism of inter-personal comparisons of utility. Issues like these called into question whether or not there was any solid philosophical grounding to judgments about policies alleged to be desirable on grounds that they could be expected to enhance the community's happiness. Many in the mainstream acknowledged the existence of these objections, but dismissed them as trivial or of little practical consequence.

There was another important fissure to an aspect of the larger program that tilted it in favor of *laissez-faire.* A presupposition that interest-group harmony prevailed was implicit in the claims made for the happy results of such a regime. This presupposition was suspect on both theoretical and empirical grounds. At the analytic level, Ricardo had demonstrated that the interests of landlords were always opposite to those of other members of the community, and Marx had founded a whole system on the basis of intrinsic disharmony. Nevertheless, there was a marked tendency for practitioners in the neo-classical mainstream to airbrush this complication out of their models and to proceed from the usual premise that a harmony of interests prevailed.

Myrdal offered a still more sweeping indictment of the orthodox theory of demand and of price formation. He called into question the realism and acceptability of standard assumptions about rationality in economic behavior. Modern psychology, he noted, had already rejected rational hedonism as a basis from which to study conduct. It was important to understand that actual behavior was influenced by a wide variety of factors, many of them non-hedonistic. Account also needed to be taken of the irrational. Part of Myrdal's critique of economic rationality is reminiscent of Thorstein Veblen's line of argument.[7]

Though Myrdal was familiar with Veblen's work when writing *The Political Element in the Development of Economic Theory,* he did not mention him in the critique of economic rationality. Instead, he suggested that Veblen was a captive of the general presuppositions of liberalism because his analysis of 'conspicuous waste' in the production process – which was brought about by producers with market power – seemed to imply that the results expected from perfect competition provided a standard of judgment. Overall, Myrdal's appraisal of Veblen in *The Political Element in the Development of Economic Theory* comes through as uncharitable and inadequately informed. But it must be remembered that the Myrdal of 1929–1930 was still in his 'pure theory' phase and hostile toward what he then understood 'institutionalism' to be all about.

The critique of two applied cases: The analysis of consumer behavior and of public finance

Myrdal rejected the concept of 'marginal utility' as used in the standard neo-classical account of the theory of demand and of price formation. The concept was immeasurable and thus smacked of objectionable metaphysics. In this connection, he walked in the footsteps of his mentor, Gustav Cassel. (Though Myrdal was highly critical of Cassel's *modus operandi* in many respects, in this instance he was a faithful disciple.) In his widely read *Theory of Social Economy*, Cassel had argued that the introduction of a metaphysical prop to explain consumer behavior was unrealistic and unnecessary. Cassel saw it as his mission to 'free the science from discussions which only too often degrade it into scholasticism of the worst kind. Such a radical purging is absolutely necessary if we wish to concentrate as far as possible on the real and undoubtedly very important problems of economic theory.'[8] For his part, Myrdal put the matter as follows:

> The new theory studies the way in which supply and demand depend upon price. . . . The theory presupposes continuity of demand and supply functions but it does not presuppose the concept of utility. Nothing need be assumed about pleasure and pain, utility and sacrifice or subjective value.[9]

In his approach to the theory of public finance, Myrdal maintained that this branch of the discipline was particularly subject to methodological traps. 'In no other field,' he wrote, 'has the intrusion of metaphysics done so much harm.'[10] Problems arose, in the first instance, because discussions of taxation and public expenditure necessarily referred not to isolated individuals, but to a larger collective. He described this as the 'communistic fiction.' The 'social housekeeping' in which these exercises were involved re-introduced the familiar problem of the validity of inter-personal comparisons of utilities. Skepticism about whether or not the required aggregation could be performed successfully directly challenged the legitimacy of statements alleging to describe the level of the community's well-being. After all, such propositions presupposed that individual utilities could be consolidated into a single sum. Similarly, it was proper to raise questions about the scientific standing of the concept of 'national income.' Some might be tempted to claim that enlargement of this aggregative construct would provide sufficient evidence to conclude that the well-being of the community had been increased. Barring the unlikely possibility that a positive change in this aggregate produced proportional improvements in the circumstances of each individual and each social group, such a conclusion would be unwarranted. As a practical matter, it was far more likely that an increment in production associated with an expansion in national income would generate non-neutral changes in the distribution of income. In consequence, it was certainly conceivable that an apparent improvement – as measured by growth in the community's income – could worsen the circumstances of some of its members. Interpreting this situation as an indicator that the community as a whole was better off would contain an implicit value judgment, namely indifference toward the consequences of a redistribution of income.

Public finance theorists who recommended policies purporting to benefit the larger community confronted a further difficulty. In all but the most trivial of cases, changes in taxing and spending programs would necessarily alter the distribution of income. This, in turn, would produce shifts in patterns of demand, resulting in changed market prices. Hence, a stable basis of comparison of national income at two points in time – that is, between the pre-change and post-change situations – was lacking. After all, the calculation of national income valued outputs at market prices, and market prices would not be the same in the two periods in question. Under these conditions, economists would be beyond their depth if they claimed a scientific and value-neutral standing for their policy recommendations.

In his further critique, Myrdal focused specifically on the writings of two Swedish economists: Knut Wicksell (whose contributions Myrdal generally admired, but whom he had not known personally) and Erik Lindahl (a friend and contemporary). This discussion, he asserted, was inspired by his judgment that 'the Swedish school of public finance probably holds the strongest theoretical position.... Wicksell and his pupil Lindahl have made the most penetrating and most consistent attempt to justify fiscal policies rationally. If nevertheless their attempt also fails, it is because they are trying to do the impossible.'[11] Presumably, Myrdal could have faulted Wicksell and Lindahl for working with 'metaphysical entities' in their use of neo-classical conceptions. He chose not to do so. For the sake of argument, he held that line of criticism in abeyance in order to analyze whether or not their chosen formulations were persuasive within their own terms.

Lindahl's treatment of the issues was then subjected to detailed inspection. It began with Lindahl's statement of the goal of the exercise:

> It is the task of this theory to elucidate the concept of justice in fiscal matters, and after an examination of the causal consequences of fiscal phenomena, to formulate the principles which apply to the various problems. An exposition of the ethical principles of taxation along those objective lines can, of course, be more or less complete, but it should be possible to arrive at agreement in principle....An objective solution along these lines is the first condition for a rational solution of practical conflicts.[12]

Lindahl then distinguished between two aspects of the larger problem. One – the 'socio-political aspect' – referred to judgments about the 'social justice of the ruling distribution of property' and these could be expected to change with shifts in the society's views. It was not the job of the fiscal theorist 'to solve the fundamental social problem, even if an objective solution were possible.' The second – described as the 'purely fiscal problem' – concerned the 'justice' of the distribution of the tax burden, and Lindahl maintained that this matter could be objectively resolved. The guiding criterion for this purpose was formulated as follows: 'The principle of taxation in the "purely fiscal sphere" consists in the requirement that the marginal value foregone through taxation should be equal to the value of the marginal public service to the taxpayer in terms of money.'[13] (There is a commendable element of originality in this stipulation. Most earlier attempts to prescribe rules for equity in taxation tended to regard government spending as 'unproductive.' Lindahl's 'principle' lent explicit legitimacy to the services provided by governments.)

In Myrdal's view, a fundamental problem remained because of interaction between the 'socio-political' aspect and the 'purely fiscal' one. In the first place, it prompted a question about the meaning of the 'correct' distribution of income and property. Society's judgment about 'correctness' referred presumably to the situation before taxes had been collected as guided by the 'purely fiscal' rule. But taxation and public expenditure in accordance with this principle would change the entire economic situation and disturb the initial distribution of income. Thus, if the pre-tax distribution were 'just,' the post-tax situation would not be so. Myrdal concluded that the 'purely fiscal' theory was 'arbitrary' and had 'no better claim to be a guide to justice than any other theory.'[14]

This conclusion, Myrdal hastened to add, did not mean that economists had nothing to contribute to informed policies in public finance. Detailed empirical studies about the incidence of taxation were badly needed. Indeed, priority should be assigned to such investigations. But economists should stop short of speculating about the 'justice' of taxing and spending policies. He called upon them to build a 'technology' of economics – one purged of valuations and metaphysics. Its proper focus would be construction of a theory of price formation from which conceptions of 'utility' (whether cardinal or ordinal) would be banned and an analysis of tax incidence sanitized from the equity considerations introduced in the standard treatments. His discussion of the 'technology' of economics, it should be noted, falls well below the standard of cogency achieved in the rest of the book. He later backed away from this position.

In the closing paragraphs of *The Political Element in the Development of Economic Theory*, Myrdal summarized the moral of the tale: 'Only if economists are modest in their claims and renounce all pretensions to postulate universal laws and norms can they promote effectively their practical objectives, viz., to keep political arguments rational, that is to say, to base them on as complete and correct a knowledge of the facts as possible. But is not the proposition that politics ought to be rational in this sense and that economists ought to support this endeavor itself a normative principle? . . . The answer to this question is that the possibility of scientific endeavour depends upon the tacit assumption that rational argument is desirable.'[15] But, to achieve rationality in economic discourse, it was incumbent on professionals to purge value-laden metaphysical conceptions from their analytic kit.

Reception of the work

Myrdal's elder Swedish colleagues were not explicitly mentioned in *The Political Element in the Development of Economic Theory* unless there was something favorable to say about them: For example, Cassel's rejection of marginal utility in the formulation of the theory of demand was commended. Yet they clearly understood that they were the target of the project. Heckscher took great and unforgiving offense. Cassel swore that he would never read the book, though he and Myrdal were able to maintain personal amiability. Wicksell, known for some iconoclasms of his own, would probably have been more sympathetic – despite the criticism of his approach to the theory of public finance – but he was no longer on the scene. One of the few notices of the work when it first appeared in Swedish was published in a Stockholm newspaper under the title 'The Rebellion of Youth.' The author was Ernst Wigforss, a leading figure in the Social Democratic party, who would later collaborate with Myrdal when both held official positions in the Swedish government.

The German edition, published in 1932, drew reviewers who commented on the parallels between Myrdal's views and those of Max Weber on the prospects for a *Wertfrei* social science and the links with Mannheim's sociology of knowledge.[16] Edward S. Mason of Harvard took note of the book's argument that mainstream economics had been 'distorted by a distinct political bias.' He added, 'This thesis is not new. What is new is its careful and scholarly examination by an able and trained economist.' Mason agreed with the author's 'general position' but 'disagree[d] rather sharply on the question of the extent to which this bias has destroyed the descriptive and explanatory value of economic theory. Myrdal appears to be unduly critical.'[17]

The first English edition, published in 1953, included an Appendix by Paul Streeten, the translator from the German, entitled 'Recent Controversies.' This valuable contribution drew attention to debates over the 'new welfare economics' in the 1930s and 1940s. As Streeten noted, formulations of the type that Myrdal had exposed as spurious were still alive and well. This was evident, for example, in the analyses of John Hicks and Nicholas Kaldor, who argued that a policy that made some members of the community better off – while others were made worse off – could still be pronounced as 'good.' The test was whether or not the gainers could compensate the losers and still be better off. (Compensation, as discussed in this context, was hypothetical, rather than actual.) I.M.D. Little's trenchant critique of this position – which argued that such claims were illegitimate because they ignored changes in the distribution of income – echoed a Myrdalian theme articulated in 1930.[18]

The English translation of 1953 attracted mixed reviews. Ludwig von Mises was unsympathetic and mistakenly identified Myrdal's critique of economic theory with the attacks leveled by the Institutionalists and by members of the German Historical School.[19] Fritz Machlup, then at Johns Hopkins University, allowed that 'there could be no serious quarrel with Myrdal's main theses that 'valuations should not be incorporated into economics by means of fallacious arguments,' that 'economic reasoning is often obscured by the fact that normative principles are not introduced explicitly,' and that 'the basic concepts are frequently charged with normative implications.' But he took issue with 'gratuitous (and misleading) remarks about 'unrealistic assumptions' and 'abstract theories...'[20] From the University of Oxford, John Hicks protested Myrdal's Cassel-derived contention that the theory of demand could be constructed 'without any assumptions about a scale of preferences, even an ordinal scale, lying behind it.' And he regarded it as unfortunate that Myrdal 'cannot even grant that maximization of real income (in any sense) is a proper economic norm.' Altogether, he lamented what he took to be a hatchet job on the edifice of received economic theory and offered an explanation: 'What he is doing here is to turn away from economics toward sociology.'[21] These reservations notwithstanding, the Nobel Prize selectors observed in 1974 that Myrdal's book *The Political Element* was a 'pioneering critique of how political values in many areas of research are inserted into economic analysis.'

Throughout his lengthy career, Myrdal remained preoccupied with the problem of objectivity in economic and social analysis. And his position shifted over time. In the Preface he prepared for the 1953 English translation, he modified his original position with regard to whether or not a 'scientific' economics could be freed of all value judgments. In his afterthoughts, he wrote,

> This implicit belief in the existence of a body of scientific knowledge acquired independently of all valuations is, as I now see it, naive empiricism. Facts do not organize themselves into concepts and theories just by being looked at.... There is an inescapable

a priori element in all scientific work. Questions must be asked before answers can be given. The questions are expressions of our interest in the world, they are at bottom valuations.'[22]

Notes

* *The Political Element in the Development of Economic Theory* went through four iterations. The original version in Swedish was published in 1930 and a German translation followed in 1932. The first English edition, translated from the German by Paul Streeten, contained an appendix on 'Recent Controversies' written by the translator and, in 1953, published by Routledge and Kegan Paul, London. (Streeten now believes that a title, reworded as follows, would be preferable: that is, *The Political Component in the Development of Economic Theory*.) A second English version, with a new introduction by Richard Swedberg, was published in 1990 by Transaction Publishers, New Brunswick, New Jersey.

1. As quoted by S. Bok, *Alva Myrdal: A Daughter's Memoir* (Reading, MA: Addison-Wesley Publishing Co., 1991), p. 79.
2. R. Swedberg, 'Introduction to the Transaction Edition,' *The Political Element in the Development of Economic Theory* (New Brunswick, NJ: Transaction Publishers, 1990), p. xviii.
3. Ibid.
4. Rockefeller Foundation Archives, Sleepy Hollow, New York.
5. G. Myrdal, 'Postscript,' *Value in Social Theory* (London: Routledge and Kegan Paul, 1958), p. 239.
6. G. Myrdal, *The Political Element in the Development of Economic Theory*, English edn, translated from the German by P. Streeten, p. 19.
7. This can be found in Veblen's *Theory of the Leisure Class* (1899) and in his article 'Why Is Economics Not an Evolutionary Science?', *Quarterly Journal of Economics*, 12 (July 1898) 373–97.
8. G. Cassel, *The Theory of Social Economy*, new revised edition translated from the 5th German edition (New York: Harcourt Brace and Co., 1932), p. 49.
9. G. Myrdal, op. cit., p. 84.
10. Ibid., p. 156.
11. G. Myrdal, *The Political Element...*, pp. 176–77. In a footnote, he paid generous tribute to Lindahl: 'I am greatly indebted to my friend Erik Lindahl for many profitable discussions of this subject. Our differences have in no way diminished the value of these discussions. If my criticism is sound and decisive, much of the credit is due to him.' (p. 238).
12. E. Lindahl, *Die Gerechtigkeit der Besteuerung*, as quoted by G. Myrdal, op. cit., pp. 177–78.
13. As quoted by G. Myrdal, op. cit., pp. 178, 181.
14. As quoted by G. Myrdal, op. cit., p. 184.

15. As quoted by G. Myrdal, op. cit., p. 206–07.
16. R. Swedberg, 'Introduction to the Transaction Edition,' pp. xxi–ii.
17. E. S. Mason, Review of 'Das politische Element in der nationalökonomischen Doktrinbildung,' *Journal of Political Economy*, 42 (April 1934) 420–21.
18. P. Streeten, 'Appendix: Recent Controversies,' *The Political Element in the Development of Economic Theory*, English edition, 1953.
19. L. von Mises, 'Myrdal's Economics,' *The Freeman* (5 April 1954) 196.
20. F. Machlup, *American Economic Review*, 45 (December 1955) 948–52.
21. J. Hicks, *Economic Journal*, 64 (December 1954) 793–95.
22. G. Myrdal, 'Preface to the English Edition,' p. xii.

3
Theorizing About Macro-Economic Instability: *Monetary Equilibrium* (versions of 1932, 1933, and 1939)

Myrdal's attack on his elders in Sweden's community of economists – as set out in *The Political Element in the Development of Economic Theory* – caused some consternation in Stockholm, but did not seriously compromise his ability to work with most of his professional colleagues. He served as a dutiful member of Gösta Bagge's team – funded by the Rockefeller Foundation in New York – that was engaged in documenting Sweden's economic history statistically.[1] Myrdal contributed a substantial volume to this enterprise, entitled *The Cost of Living in Sweden, 1830–1930*, that was published in 1933. Though he had reservations about the quality of the data with which he had been obliged to work, he drew some satisfaction from his attempt to transcend the limitations of the raw material. In addition, he contributed a major essay – dealing with migration from the countryside to urban areas in Sweden since the mid-nineteenth century – to a volume honoring Gustav Cassel on the occasion of his retirement in 1933.[2]

Myrdal's most significant analytic work in the early 1930s, however, was oriented in a quite different direction. He and Alva (both as recipients of Rockefeller Foundation Fellowships) had arrived in the United States at the moment the stock market crash in 1929 triggered the onset of the Great Depression. In the months that followed, they observed firsthand the massive economic distress and disruption created in its wake. Events then posed a fundamental challenge to economists who were pressed to explain how this catastrophe could have happened and how a future recurrence could be prevented. Orthodox economic theory at the time was not well equipped for these tasks. After all, standard doctrine held that lapses from full employment would be temporary and self-correcting. This view was distinctly at odds with the observable reality.

Myrdal joined this discussion in an article appearing in *Ekonomisk tidskrift* entitled 'Om penningteoretisk jämvikt.'[3] A revised German translation was published in 1933 in a volume edited by Friedrich A. Hayek.[4] According to the original plan, the space that Myrdal's contribution occupied in this volume was to be filled by a submission from Lindahl. The latter, however, was unable to deliver a manuscript on a timely basis and suggested Myrdal as a substitute. Reportedly, Hayek was opposed to Myrdal's argument and its policy implications, but reluctantly accepted it for publication.[5] An English translation – with a few modifications – appeared under the title *Monetary Equilibrium* in 1939.[6]

The structure of *Monetary Equilibrium*

Myrdal maintained that the 'main purpose' of his excursion into monetary theory was to 'include anticipations in the monetary system.'[7] In his judgment, recent contributions to discourse on monetary analysis had failed to incorporate this issue. He cited in particular the works of Friedrich Hayek and John Maynard Keynes. (The Keynes reference, it should be noted, was to his *Treatise on Money*, published in 1930.) Both authors were faulted because there was 'no place for the uncertainty factor or for anticipations' in their theoretical systems.[8]

For Myrdal, as for his Swedish contemporaries, it came naturally to address the problem of macro-economic equilibrium within the framework inherited from Wicksell. In the latter's account, aggregative economic fluctuations could be traced to discrepancies between the 'natural' rate of interest – that is, one that equilibrated saving and investment – and the 'market' rate of interest. In a situation in which the 'natural' rate exceeded the 'market' rate, borrowing for investment in capital goods would be stimulated. If these relationships were reversed, economic contraction would follow. Myrdal had to approach the conception of a 'natural' rate of interest somewhat gingerly. After all, Wicksell's formulations on this matter looked suspiciously like the metaphysical entities that Myrdal had denounced so roundly in *The Political Element in the Development of Economic Theory*. He was certainly sensitive to this complication: Throughout this work, references to the 'natural' rate were enclosed in inverted commas. And he spoke to the larger issue by quoting Wagemann's critique of Wicksell and his own response to it:

> Wagemann writes about Wicksell's monetary theory: 'The empirically established facts, in this as in other cases, are obscured rather than explained by "theory". For it is, after all, pure metaphysics to say that interest rates have to correspond to the "natural rate of interest" on capital. . . . Nothing can be explained by the mystic notions of this theory.'

Myrdal commented on this position:

> Wagemann is objectively quite correct. Wicksell's 'natural rate' does not belong to this world. . . . But the question is whether one cannot arrive, by a perfection of the Wicksellian train of thought, at statements of problems which can be useful not only in explaining the 'empirically established facts' but even in their very observation. 'Facts' are by no means easily palpable things, especially if they are of a rather general and complex character. Behind each formulation of 'facts' are extensive theoretical hypotheses.[9]

Myrdal developed his treatment of monetary equilibrium as an 'immanent criticism' of Wicksell's contribution. By no means did this imply a blanket endorsement of Wicksell's views and it certainly did not preclude the introduction of Myrdalian innovations. What it did mean was that Wicksell's formulation served as a point of departure. On one point, however, Myrdal absorbed Wicksell without significant modification, namely the conception of a 'cumulative process.' With respect to the problem at hand, this could be defined as a '*dynamic deviation in one direction or the other from a monetary equilibrium*.'[10] And he added that 'the essential feature of the process is a shift in production which brings with it an increased production of real capital if the dynamic process has an upward direction, and a decreased production if the process has a downward trend.'[11]

Consider, for example, the case when the 'natural' rate exceeded the money rate of interest. Credit would then be perceived as being cheap, and profit expectations as bullish. This state of affairs would stimulate businesses to borrow and spend on capital formation. This behavior, in turn, would generate upward pressure on prices, reinforcing the view that still more attractive profit opportunities could be expected. The cumulative principle could be observed in action, Myrdal wrote, 'When the entrepreneurs begin to anticipate future price rises, as must happen sooner or later if the money rate of interest is not increased, then the process gets wind behind its sails and moves faster and faster.'[12]

Myrdal brought to the table here a novel terminology to enrich understanding of the crucial role of expectations in determining the performance of the macro-economy. His approach was clearly a consistent extension of the emphasis he had assigned to expectations as a factor in price formation, the central theme that he had elaborated in his doctoral dissertation. *Monetary Equilibrium,* in its second iteration, introduced a fresh vocabulary to distinguish the results savers and investors anticipated from those that actually eventuated. The usage *ex ante* referred to the expected or planned outcomes that affected decision-making by savers and investors, whereas *ex post* referred to actual magnitudes of saving and investment that were observable after the fact. These expressions did not appear in the original Swedish version. They were added in the German translation of 1933 at the suggestion of Myrdal's friend and translator, Gerhard MacKenroth.[13] In the English version of 1939, Myrdal wrote, 'Probably the chief contribution of this essay, if any, is to have originated the concepts of *ex ante* and *ex post*; and to have emphasized the importance of clearly recognizing the period implicit in monetary analysis.'[14] *Ex ante* and *ex post* were quickly assimilated into the standard kit of macro-economic theorists.

The next step in the argument turned on a recognition that – in advanced capitalist economies – decisions to save and decisions to invest were, for the most part, made by different people. Anyone with an income could make a savings decision by refraining from consumption spending. Decisions to spend on capital goods, by contrast, were made by a far more limited segment of the population: that is, businessmen. There was certainly no guarantee that the plans of the public to withhold from consumption would match the amounts sought by businesses for capital disposal. When a mismatch occurred, a condition of monetary disequilibrium arose that would generate fluctuations in incomes and prices. And this disequilibrium would persist until *ex ante* saving matched *ex ante* investment. This should be sharply differentiated from the condition of *ex post* saving and investment. As a bookkeeping matter, these magnitudes would be the same after the fact, a situation brought about by changes in incomes and prices on the amounts actually saved. In subsequent accounts of the *ex post* identity – notably, the one offered in John Maynard Keynes's *General Theory of Employment, Interest, and Money* – emphasis was placed on unintended changes in investment in inventory as the balancing item in response to disequilibrium. This explanation was absent from Myrdal's *Monetary Equilibrium*.

The role of monetary policy

Myrdal regarded monetary theory as an aid to intelligent policy-making. But this prompted a formidable question: As a practical matter, how effective could monetary policy be expected to be? He took the Central Bank's manipulation of the discount rate to be its primary policy instrument. But, he emphasized, circumstances in the real world might blunt – if not counteract altogether – the realization of the outcome that the Central Bank was attempting to accomplish. He invited consideration of the response to credit stringency when policy-makers raised the discount rate with the intent of applying downward pressure on prices and incomes.

In these circumstances, various factors intervened to impede this process. Myrdal noted, for instance, the stickiness of wage rates – especially in the component of the labor force that was unionized – and the general reluctance of workers to accept a decline in pay. In addition, firms with the market power to administer prices were under little pressure to respond to a tightening of discount rates. Other institutional factors were at work as well. Many firms would resist cutting their payouts in dividends, lest it 'spoil their chances of raising capital in the future,' even though their net income had fallen. There was a stickiness as well in salaries paid to highly skilled employees in the commercial and technical sectors, as well as in the civil service. He attached considerable weight to a further consideration, namely that 'the consuming habits of the upper and middle classes [were] fairly stabilized' and they could be expected to resist an erosion in their standard of living. He elaborated on this point as follows:

> This is quite natural, both in view of the greater feeling of economic security of these social classes . . . and in view of their greater adherence to social conventions (a very important part of their consumption is, notoriously, of a 'social' character, that it is based on matters of prestige) . . .[15]

This line of argument could have come directly out of Thorstein Veblen's *Theory of the Leisure Class*, with its emphasis on the behavioral conditioning associated with 'conspicuous consumption.'[16]

The upshot of all this was the conclusion that 'a uniform loosening or tightening of the whole standard combination of credit conditions often need not lead to a Wicksellian cumulative process . . . .'[17] To the extent that stickiness in wages and administered prices was responsible for this outcome, Myrdal could have called for an attack on market power, whether exercised by firms or by organized labor. He did not do so. Economists elsewhere – particularly in the United States – were then insisting that wage–price inflexibility was responsible for the persistence of Depression and that a regime of wage–price flexibility would provide the remedy. Myrdal did not follow their lead. The point of the analytical exercise he had performed was to highlight the limited effectiveness of monetary policy.

This definitely did not mean that policy interventions were futile. To the contrary, informed policy-making was essential to the achievement of monetary equilibrium at a high level of production and employment. On this matter, he observed,

> Maintaining a monetary equilibrium becomes a question not only of monetary policy but of economic policy as a whole, social policy and the institutions which rule the labour market, cartel legislation and all related factors.[18]

Nevertheless, he pointed out that 'in an economy in which a socialistic centralization of all economic policy has not yet been carried through, an "isolation" of monetary policy from other economic policy exists as an institutional fact.'[19]

Myrdal's exploration of these issues yielded another important analytic finding, namely that monetary equilibrium – as established by an equality between *ex ante* savings and *ex ante* investment – could be achieved at quite different absolute values for the discount rate or the price level. There was certainly no implication here that a state of monetary equilibrium coincided with one of maximum employment. To the contrary, an underemployment equilibrium was both thinkable and observable in a depressed economy. Myrdal and the Keynes of *The General Theory* were on the same page here, though their analytic procedures were markedly different.

Assessments of the achievement

Pre-1939 – in the absence of an English translation – Myrdal's analysis of macro-economic instability received little attention in the wider world. With a few exceptions, contemporaries in the community of English-speaking economists failed to appreciate its message. In the version published in German in 1933, Myrdal had taken note of an obstacle to the international transmission of innovative economic ideas that originated in Sweden. In England, he remarked, Wicksell's line of analysis was imperfectly understood. He then described D. H. Robertson's *Banking and the Price Level* as a 'significant little book' but 'he, too, obviously lacks a thorough knowledge of Wicksell and his pupils, and he has therefore been forced unnecessarily to think for himself.' Myrdal added,

> J. M. Keynes' new, brilliant, though not always clear, work *A Treatise on Money*, is completely permeated by Wicksell's influence. Nevertheless Keynes' work, too, suffers somewhat from the attractive Anglo-Saxon kind of unnecessary originality, which has its roots in certain systematic gaps in the knowledge of the German language on the part of the majority of English economists.[20]

One British reader of the German translation, however, was mightily impressed. John R. Hicks, then at the London School of Economics and a future Nobel Prize winner in economics, reviewed the book for *Economica*. He observed that 'there can be no question at all that [Myrdal's] work marks a very definite step in advance. It is even one of those books one feels loath to criticize, for fear that one's criticisms may perhaps deter some reader from examining the book itself – and that would be a disaster.' Hicks cut to the crux of the matter by identifying the fundamental issues turning on the *ex ante* and *ex post* conceptions of saving and investment.[21] Reflecting in the 1980s on his 1934 review, Hicks wrote, 'I now feel that I wrote that review too soon, since it does not yet show how much I learned, and was to learn, from Myrdal.' He added, '. . . though I praised the book highly, I have come to feel that I did not praise it highly enough.'[22] He further observed that his study of Myrdal equipped him to grasp easily the message of Keynes's *General Theory.* Nicholas Kaldor – who was also at the London School of Economics when the German edition appeared – reported that, through Hicks, he was 'put on the track (among others) of the younger Swedish economists, particularly Myrdal, who first made me realise the shortcomings of the "monetarist" approach of the Austrian School of von Mises and von Hayek and made me such an easy convert to Keynes after the appearance of the *General Theory* three years later.'[23]

When the English translation of *Monetary Equilibrium* appeared in 1939 – 3 years after the publication of Keynes's *General Theory of Employment, Interest, and Money* – reviewers quite naturally were inclined to draw comparisons between the two works. Writing from Cambridge University, Joan Robinson took note of Myrdal's remark on the 'attractive Anglo-Saxon kind of unnecessary originality' on the part of Keynes and Robertson, who 'discovered for themselves many ideas already worked out by Wicksell.' She further noted that the Swedish economists enjoyed advantages 'in the freedom that Wicksell won for them from the tyranny of Say's Law and the Quantity Theory of Money.' They were further advantaged by the fact that 'Wicksell succeeded in raising a generation of pupils who regarded criticism of the master as their first duty.' And she cited Pigou's comment that 'among Marshall's pupils reverence for the master checked enterprise and initiative.' Robinson also noted that Myrdal's monetary equilibrium could be achieved at any level of economic activity and 'certainly prevails at the bottom of a slump.' This suggested that Myrdal's 'own argument' demonstrated that monetary equilibrium was a 'matter of secondary importance.' After all, the issue of primary importance to the Cambridge School – that is, the achievement and maintenance of full employment – did not come through as such in Myrdal's analysis. He was criticized for holding that 'a certain amount of unemployment [was] necessary and desirable in order to prevent the continuous rise of money wages and prices which comes about when the "monopoly position" of the workers is too strong.'[24]

In a brief notice appearing in *The American Economic Review*, Paul Samuelson welcomed the appearance of this 'important essay' which made available the 'thought of the virile Swedish school' to English readers. He lamented, however, the lapse of time since the original publication in Swedish, during which the 'center of interest and emphasis in monetary theory has veered away from the Wicksellian analysis.' He identified 'fundamental inadequacies . . . from more recent points of view,' such as 'an undue emphasis upon the importance of price and interest rate movements as compared to those of output and employment . . . .' And he added that 'most important is the lack of realization that monetary equilibrium in the author's sense could conceivably involve 50 per cent unemployment . . .'[25]

Robinson and Samuelson obviously read *Monetary Equilibrium* through Keynesian lenses. So also did Abba P. Lerner, then at the University of Virginia. He maintained that 'it is unfair to the English and American economist who cannot read Swedish (and doesn't read German) and who has been tantalized with tales of how far ahead the Swedes are of all other economists. It is much more seriously unfair to the authors to have their wares shown only after their essence has already reached the public by indirect routes so that the originals look second-hand and rather faded. This unfortunate result is especially apparent in the present case because of the great advance made by Mr J. M. Keynes, to whose genius in moulding the vague reverberations of Swedish thought into a systematic scheme these republications pay unintended but impressive homage.'[26]

From Myrdal's perspective, a substantially more sympathetic appraisal emerged from the pen of Howard Ellis, then at the University of California. Writing in the *Journal of Political Economy*, he expected that Myrdal's volume would 'seriously challenge the current dominant theory evolved by Keynes.' Elaborating on this theme, he observed that 'unlike Keynes's, Myrdal's equilibrium at less than full employment does not involve, or at least does not require (1) the continuous absorption of saving into hoards or dissipation by attempts to hoard; (2) an inelastic demand schedule for capital; and (3) the cessation of net investment.' He added,

> In as much as these features of the Keynesian system have been the object of greatest skepticism, a theory which offers an explanation of persisting unemployment without them, and at the same time takes account of the apparent discouragement to investment entailed by savings in a depression, merits careful attention.'

He regarded Myrdal's 'results' as 'simply more convincing.'[27]

Without question, the most enthusiastic reading of Myrdal's contribution came from Britain's G. L. S. Shackle. In his view, 'there were to be found in Myrdal's essay which appeared in 1933 a number of new ideas, forming parts of a precise and coherent whole, which have become part of the most essential and characteristic frame of modern economic dynamics, which have become associated, in the minds of English economists at least, with names other than their true author's. It is not too much, in my opinion, to claim for Myrdal's essay an originality and path-breaking importance equal to anything that appeared in economics in the period between the two wars . . . '[28] There was a clear implication here that Myrdal had preceded and trumped Keynes.[29]

Schumpeter was of a similar mind. He credited Myrdal – in company with Swedish colleagues Erik Lindahl, Bertil Ohlin, and Erik Lundberg – with leading a post-Wicksellian development '. . . that paralleled and in some important points anticipated the English (Keynesian) one without becoming known to English economists.'[30]

A counterfactual question

If Myrdal had pressed for an English translation of his work on macro-economic instability before 1936, would the world subsequently refer to a 'Myrdalian revolution,' or to a 'Myrdal-Keynes revolution,' rather than to an exclusively 'Keynesian revolution' in economic theory? Perhaps, but not likely. The Wicksellian framework was organized around instabilities in the general price level, rather than changes in aggregate output and employment, as was the case in the Keynesian formulation. The latter issues had far greater salience in the

Great Depression than the former ones. In addition, Keynes – unlike Myrdal – addressed the question of the demand for money (which introduced the possibility of hoarding and a 'liquidity trap'). This ingenious conception had major explanatory power with respect to the accumulation of excess reserves in the commercial banking system in the 1930s, especially in the United States. This bit of theorizing was absent from the analyses of Myrdal and the other Swedish post-Wicksellians.

In an interview in 1982, Myrdal was asked to comment on why he had not pushed for an English translation in 1933 and he responded as follows:

> I wrote in Swedish for Swedes and to some extent for Scandinavians and I was not particularly concerned that my thoughts did not reach an international audience.... I remember that I received an invitation from the International Labor Bureau to publish in their journal a translated version of my appendix to the Social Democratic government's budget that was presented in January 1933. However, I declined the invitation on the grounds that I was fully preoccupied with work in Sweden and did not wish to have the trouble of proofreading a translation.[31]

But what should one make of the broader issue of claims to analytic priorities on the part of champions of the Stockholm School, on the one hand, and the Keynesians, on the other? This topic has spawned a bulky literature, with Ohlin as the lead spokesman for the Swedish camp and Don Patinkin for the Keynesians.[32] Bo Gustafsson's characterization of this debate as 'a perennial of doctrinal history' is on target.[33] It would be idle to pretend that this controversy will be resolved by consensus any time soon.

On another matter, however, it is possible to speak with assurance: the reception Keynes received when visiting Stockholm shortly after the publication of his *General Theory*. On 1 October 1936, he delivered a lecture in Stockholm as the guest of the Political Economy Club. According to the minutes of the meeting, his subject was 'My grounds for departure from orthodox economic traditions.' Those present included Gunnar Myrdal, Bertil Ohlin, Erik Lundberg, and Dag Hammarskjöld. Ohlin reportedly informed Keynes that Stockholm School members had read *The General Theory* 'with the joy of recognition.' The discussion following the lecture went on until midnight, with younger Swedish economists criticizing Keynes 'for being too classical.'[34]

In view of the standing and significance of *Monetary Equilibrium*, it remains a mystery why the Swedish Academy neglected to mention it in the citation prepared in connection with the award of Myrdal's Nobel Memorial Prize in Economics in 1974.

Notes

1. For background on the Rockefeller Foundation's support for economic research in Sweden, see E. Craven, 'Gösta Bagge, the Rockefeller Foundation and Empirical Social Science Research in Sweden, 1924–1940,' *The Stockholm School of Economics Revisitied*, L. Jonung, ed. (Cambridge and New York: Cambridge University Press, 1991), pp. 79–97. As it happened, Bagge's first visit to the Rockefeller Foundation's headquarters in New York in September 1924 coincided with the first day on the job for a new director, Beardsley Ruml. Later in this story, Ruml figures again as instrumental in recruiting Myrdal to head the study of the Negro problem in the United States, a project that ultimately produced *An American Dilemma* in 1944.
2. See G. Myrdal, 'Industrialization and Population,' *Economic Essays in Honour of Gustav Cassel* (London: George Allen and Unwin, Ltd, 1933), pp. 435–57.
3. Though written in 1932, this essay was published in an issue of *Ekonomisk tidskrift* dated as 1931. It appears that there was a publication lag in the production of this journal.
4. See G. Myrdal, 'Der Gleichgewichtsberiff als Instrument der geldtheoretischen Analyse,' *Beträge zur Geldtheorie*, F. A. Hayek, ed., Vienna, 1933.
5. See N. Shehadi, 'The LSE and the Stockholm School in the 1930s' (New York and Cambridge: Cambridge University Press, 1991), L. Jonung, ed., p. 382.
6. Tord Palander has identified the emendations between translations in 'On the Concepts and Methods of the "Stockholm School,"' *International Economic Papers*, 3 (London and New York: Macmillan, 1953).
7. G. Myrdal, *Monetary Equilibrium* (London: William Hodge and Company, 1939), p. 32.
8. Ibid.
9. Ibid., p. 48n.
10. Ibid., p. 29.
11. Ibid., p. 34
12. Ibid., p. 25.
13. On this point, see L. Jonung (ed.), *The Stockholm School of Economics Revisited* (Cambridge and New York: Cambridge University Press, 1991), p. 29. R. G. H. Henriksson's commentary on this transaction merits note,

'. . . the German translator . . . introduced the passwords of the Stockholm School, *ex ante* and *ex post,* as convenient substitutes for some of Myrdal's verbal equilibristics in the Swedish text . . . . Generally, rigor and comprehension are lost in translation, but in the case of Swedish authors, sometimes the opposite occurred.' See Henriksson, 'The Political Economy Club,' in Jonung (ed.), op. cit., p. 62.

14. G. Myrdal, *Monetary Equilibrium*, p. 47.
15. Ibid., pp. 165–66.
16. Myrdal's point here was echoed in J. Duesenberry's *Income, Savings, and the Theory of Consumer Behavior* (Cambridge, MA: Harvard University Press, 1949).
17. G. Myrdal, op. cit., p. 183.
18. Ibid., p. 184.
19. Ibid., p. 185.
20. Ibid., pp. 8–9. In the German edition of 1933, this passage appeared on p. 370.
21. Hicks's review appeared in the November 1934 issue of *Economica* and has been printed in J. R. Hicks, *Money, Interest and Wages: Collected Essays on Economic Theory,* II (Cambridge, MA: Harvard University Press, 1982), pp. 42–45.
22. Ibid., pp. 8, 42.
23. N. Kaldor, 'Recollections of an Economist,' *Banca Nazionale del Lavoro Quarterly Review* (March 1986), 7 (as quoted in Shehadi, op. cit.).
24. J. Robinson, 'Review of Myrdal's *Monetary Equilibrium,' Economic Journal,* 49 (September 1939), 493–95.
25. P. Samuelson, 'Review of Myrdal's *Monetary Equilibrium,' American Economic Review,* 30 (March 1940) 129–30.
26. A. P. Lerner, 'Some Swedish Stepping Stones in Economic Theory,' *Canadian Journal of Economics and Political Science,* 6 (November 1940) 574–91. In this review article, Lerner was commenting on both Myrdal's *Monetary Equilibrium* and Lindahl's *Studies in the Theory of Money and Capital.*
27. H. Ellis, 'Review of Myrdal's *Monetary Equilibrium,' Journal of Political Economy,* 48 (June 1940) 434–46.
28. G. L. S. Shackle, 'Myrdal's Analysis of *Monetary Equilibrium,' Oxford Economic Papers,* 7 (March 1945) 47–66.
29. On this point, Shackle was more explicit in 1967, when he wrote, 'Myrdal worked out with exact logic a theory where subtle and elusive difficulties are recognized and coped with . . . . In all but its assignments of emphasis, *Monetary Equilibrium* anticipated Keynes's *General Theory,* though not conveying Keynes's sense of revolutionary achievement and conviction of power.' (G. L. S. Shackle, *The Years of High Theory: Invention and Tradition in Economic Thought, 1926–1939,* Cambridge University Press, 1967, p. 98.)
30. J. A. Schumpeter, *History of Economic Analysis* (Oxford University Press, 1954), p. 1085.
31. As reported by Jonung, op. cit., p. 28.

32. A few illustrative examples will suffice. Ohlin set this debate in motion with two articles that appeared in the *Economic Journal*, 47: 'Some Notes on the Stockholm Theory of Savings and Investment - I' (March 1937) 53–69, and 'Some Notes on the Stockholm Theory of Savings and Investment - II' (June 1937) 221–40. Ohlin is also responsible for introducing the label 'Stockholm School.' Exchanges with Patinkin date from the collection edited by Patinkin and J. C. Leith, *Keynes, Cambridge, and the General Theory* (London: Macmillan, 1977) to which Ohlin contributed a chapter entitled 'Some Comments on Keynesianism and the Swedish School before 1935.' Discussions continued in the *Scandinavian Journal of Economics*, 80 (1978). Patinkin's 'Some Observations on Ohlin's 1933 Article,' *History of Political Economy*, 10 (Fall 1978) 413–19, is also pertinent.
33. See B. Gustafsson, 'A Perennial of Doctrinal History,' *Economy and History*, XVI, 1973.
34. As reported by R. G. H. Henriksson, 'The Political Economy Club and the Stockholm School, 1917–1951,' in Jonung, op. cit., p. 41. Keynes's remarks on this occasion were later developed into an essay that appeared in *The Lessons of Monetary Experience: Essays in Honor of Irving Fisher*, A. D. Gayer, ed. (New York: Farrar and Rinehart, Inc., 1937), under the title 'The Theory of the Rate of Interest,' pp. 145–52.

4
Structuring Counter-Cyclical Fiscal Policies in the 1930s

Myrdal formally joined Sweden's Social Democratic Party in 1932. He marked the occasion by writing an essay entitled 'The Dilemma of Social Policy' – which he described as a 'moral' one. (There is an arresting symmetry in his choice of language here and the usages he later deployed. In 1944, one of the crowning achievements of his career was the publication of *An American Dilemma: The Negro Problem and Modern Democracy*, which he then diagnosed as a 'moral' issue.)

His 1932 essay, intended to promote the interests of the Social Democrats, read more like a university seminar paper than a political tract. He traced the evolution of the classical liberal posture toward social policy over the past century. This tradition had been rooted in beliefs that government intervention was virtually always suspect. This view had moderated somewhat over the course of the nineteenth century when it became widely recognized that the state should properly provide relief to members of the community suffering from extreme distress. The liberal ideology, however, had become trapped in a dilemma because it still endorsed the 'utility and necessity of individual responsibility.' It thus distrusted social policies that 'could lessen pressures on the individual to be self-sufficient through thrift, prudence, and entrepreneurship.' When confronted with the crisis of depression-scale unemployment, the classical liberal perspective was inadequate and paralyzed by the fact that 'helping the unemployed sometimes not only lessens their interest in looking for work, but above all strengthens the unions in their attempts to constantly raise wages . . . . (E)rgo: unemployment help has caused more unemployment.'[1] Myrdal further maintained that 'the upper and middle classes are beginning to lose faith in the societal order on top of which they are floating. And this happens at about the same time as social policies reached the limit where even the more reform-willing within these classes feel that they can't in good conscience reach further.'[2]

A dilemma was also imbedded in the socialistic point of view. Socialist reformers had concentrated on unemployment in the current crisis. This was the 'road of least resistance,' but it failed to come to grips with a fundamental problem. Social policies in current circumstances, Myrdal insisted, could serve as 'oil on troubled waters' only when their benefits were continuously augmented. But, with 'liberal upper-class interest in further extension of social policy... dampened,' the situation was ripe for a 'radicalization of labor opinion.' There was a risk that workers would come to view all social policies as 'just patches on the rags' and to focus their attention on more profound changes in 'the system.'[3]

In Myrdal's view, remedies to these dilemmas should be sought by harnessing the talents of experts to address defined social problems, such as unemployment. This approach was more radical than that of the socialist reformers, though it stopped well short of 'all-round revolution.' It was not premised on egalitarianism as an objective, though some leveling of incomes and wealth might follow from measures dealing with specific social ills – for example, the housing needs of the poorer classes. What this added up to was a call for expertly led economic planning. The Social Democratic party came to power in the election of 1932 and was to remain the party of government in Sweden for the next four decades. Myrdal had now established his credentials as an 'insider.'

Work with the committee on unemployment

In March 1932, Myrdal was appointed as a member of an official Committee on Unemployment. In one iteration or another, this Committee had been in being since 1927. Its work had initially focused on the nature and causes of long-term unemployment and some valuable statistical documentation was produced on this topic. With the onset of the Great Depression, the emphasis understandably shifted to the study of cyclical unemployment and its remedies. In the latter phase of this undertaking, Myrdal and his fellow neo-Wicksellians were largely in command of the project. Bertil Ohlin conducted investigations of 'monetary policy, public works, subsidies and tariff policy as remedies for unemployment.' Other participants included Erik Lindahl, Alf Johansson, and Dag Hammarskjöld. The contribution of Ernst Wigforss, a Social Democratic politician, deserves particular mention. Though an amateur economist, he was very well read in the literature and in touch with the latest economic thinking in Britain as well as in Sweden. He was a force on the Committee and his academic colleagues accorded him the signal honor of election to Stockholm's Political Economy Club.[4] (It is worth noting in passing that Wigforss, with a doctorate in linguistics, did have impressive academic credentials.)

With the accession of the Social Democratic Party to power, Ernst Wigforss became the Minister of Finance. For Myrdal, a new collaborative opportunity was thus opened up. Its first fruit became visible early in 1933 when Wigforss asked Myrdal to produce a memorandum on the case for an expansionist fiscal policy. This 45-page document, entitled *Konjuktur och offentlig hushållning* (Business Cycles and Public Finance), was attached as Appendix III to Wigforss's Budget Message to the Swedish Parliament in January 1933.

The more complete – and, at 279 pages, much longer – statement of this argument emerged in early 1934 in a study Myrdal prepared under the auspices of the Committee on Unemployment with the title *Finanspolitikens ekonomiska verkningar* (The Economic Effects of Fiscal Policy). This document was more akin to an academic monograph than to the typical state paper. In it, Myrdal spoke directly to the concerns of those who held annually balanced budgets to be central to 'sound' public finance. He first drew attention to the fact that the government's revenues were reduced because of a shrinking tax base in a depressed economy. This tended to push the budget into deficit, though it was an unintended one. Conventional orthodoxy would prescribe its standard remedies: a tax increase, a reduction in governmental spending programs, or some combination of the two. That response, he argued, would make matters worse: It would have the effect of reducing aggregate spending when its enlargement was needed to stimulate recovery. What the situation called for was an expansionary policy built around loan-financed governmental spending on useful public works. This would have an immediate impact on employment and incomes by virtue of the government's spending initiative. But the expansionary process would not end there. Workers and suppliers of materials for public works projects would spend most, if not all, of their increased income, thus stimulating employment in the consumer goods sector. Myrdal clearly was in command of a conception of an investment-income multiplier. By comparison with R. F. Kahn's formulation in the *Economic Journal* of 1931, it lacked only a specification of the conditions under which the multiplier process would be brought to a halt.[5]

Other features of Myrdal's proposed program were notable. The actual impact on the government's finances would be substantially lower than the outlays allocated to public works proper. Re-employed workers on these projects would otherwise have made claims on the budget in the form of unemployment relief. Calculation of the net costs should make adjustment for what had been saved in payments of a dole. Allocations for public works were superior to the dole for two other reasons. They added to the nation's stock of useful public assets, whereas transfer payments for unemployment relief would leave nothing behind to show for them. In addition, engagement in useful work – as opposed to being the recipient of a handout – would contribute much to bracing morale among workers.

Myrdal also reminded his readers that expansion in income and employment stemming from the public works program would itself tend to narrow the initial deficit by widening the tax base, thus enabling the Treasury to capture additional revenues. As the economy approached a full capacity level of operations, budget surpluses could be expected. These funds, in turn, would offset the deficit incurred when it was necessary to get the economy moving. What he had in mind here was a strategy of a budget balanced over the course of a business cycle. But these outcomes would be possible only if the straitjacket of annually balanced budgets – without regard to the condition of the economy – were discarded. He hoped also to see another budgetary innovation put in place, namely a two-part budget separated into a current account and a capital account. Denmark, he noted, had pioneered this procedure. (Sweden was to adopt it in 1936.)

Myrdal was well aware that an expansionary fiscal program would need to reckon with a potential constraint: a risk that it might induce severe drains on a country's foreign exchange reserves. He sketched a number of ways to deal with that threat by distinguishing between three possible sets of circumstances. In Scenario 1, he identified steps that might widen 'international space' while simultaneously stimulating the domestic economy. These included moderate devaluation of the currency, plus import duties and export subsidies. Scenario 2 dealt with measures to widen 'international space' that were neutral in their domestic impact. Increased capital imports and decreased capital exports fell into this category, as did a program of modest wage cuts that benefitted some employers with lower costs, but were offset by injury to other producers who experienced reduced demand for their products. Scenario 3 – which examined widened 'international space' accomplished by depressing the home economy – was by far the least attractive. *In extremis,* this might require increased taxes to shrink demand for consumer goods and reduction in wages paid by the state and other public bodies. This was clearly an outcome to be avoided. Myrdal thus recognized that a balance-of-payments constraint could be at odds with an expansionary program. Should such a problem arise, it was self-evidently preferable if it could be dealt within the framework of Scenario 1.[6]

Pursuing an expansionist fiscal policy, 1933–1936

With a Social Democratic government installed in power by 1933 – and with Ernst Wigforss as its Finance Minister – the stage was set for a trial run in expansionary fiscal policy. According to his estimates, Sweden's national income had fallen from roughly 8.3 billion kronor in 1930 to 7.0 billion by 1933.[7] Meanwhile, unemployment had increased sharply. In the first quarter of 1933, applicants for public assistance through the Unemployment Commission numbered 186,000, and 28.4 percent of trade union members were reported as unemployed.[8]

The new government responded by expanding appropriations for public works projects. Major enlargement in spending on capital projects deemed to be 'unproductive' – those that did not generate self-liquidating revenue – was mounted. Outlays in this category rose from 15.1 million kronor in the fiscal year ending 30 June 1934 (the last budget year for which the preceding government had been responsible) to 105.1 million kronor in fiscal 1935, and to 207.7 million kronor in fiscal 1936. Capital spending in the 'productive' category also increased, though much less dramatically. The structure of the Swedish economy – in which the state functioned as an entrepreneur in the railway, electric power, post and telegraph, mining, and forestry sectors – lent itself to governmentally managed guidance on counter-cyclical investment policies. Some dissatisfaction was expressed, however, with regard to foot-dragging on the part of managers of state enterprises.[9]

The upshot of this activity was increased deficits in the public accounts which, this time, were deliberate rather than unintended (as was the case with the former government). Loan-financed activities, however, were not impressively large: In fiscal 1934, they accounted for just under 11 percent of central government expenditures, and in fiscal 1935, this magnitude was slightly less than 12 percent. In fiscal 1936, a budgetary surplus was recorded.[10] Simultaneously, the ranks of the unemployed shrank substantially and the volume of employment grew. By 1936, the index of employed workers (with 1929 = 100) was two points above the level of 1929 and 17 points above the level of 1933.[11]

Wigforss could quite reasonably draw satisfaction from these outcomes. He stopped short of claiming that the expansionary fiscal policy was primarily responsible for these results. He did pronounce the program as a success when success was measured against his suggested criterion, namely its acceptance by public opinion. 'The only distinction of practical importance,' he wrote in 1938, 'is how the experience of past years should influence future action. If the question is put in this way, one ventures to say a preponderant majority of the general public and of experts in these matters consider the experience so favorable that there should be future experimentation along the lines of "the new fiscal policy".'[12] And he added that part of the public's acceptance of this policy could be attributed to the commitment to offset deficits in the lean years with surpluses in the fat ones. This re-specification of fiscal 'soundness' was crucial to the maintenance of public confidence and should not be compromised.

Myrdal spoke to this episode in a paper presented at the annual meetings of the American Economic Association in December 1938. He regarded the Swedish experiment as a useful 'laboratory,' but asserted that 'the policy was carried out only half-heartedly.'[13] In his view, the program had suffered because capital projects had not been prepared in advance, had begun too late for maximum impact, and were smaller in scale than ideally would have been desired. A central lesson to be learned here was that advance planning of worthwhile public projects should be set in motion as a buffer against a future recession or depression. He recognized that, potentially, Sweden was advantageously situated to mount counter-cyclical fiscal policies by virtue of the substantial weight of state enterprises in total economic activity. There was, however, a 'practical difficulty in that managers of state enterprises are apt to react very much as managers of private enterprises. The management of state railroads, for example, is naturally most interested in investment when traffic is increasing and actually creating new needs. But the managers of state enterprises ought to be more easily educated, and, in the last instance, they are under political control, which private investment is not.'[14]

Myrdal echoed Wigforss in emphasizing the imperative of balancing the public accounts over the course of a business cycle. But he also drew attention to a technique that could preserve a commitment to fiscal 'soundness,' while maximizing the flexibility that policy-makers could enjoy when mounting a stimulative spending program. This was made possible by Sweden's adoption of the Danish scheme for dividing the budget into two components: that is, a current or 'running' account in which expenditures had to be matched by receipts; and a capital account in which self-liquidating investments could be financed by borrowing. These principles, he maintained, were now generally accepted as 'sound.' Within this framework, added scope for policy maneuver could be obtained by adjustments that permitted 'unproductive' (or non-self-liquidating) capital spending to be re-defined as 'productive' and thereby eligible for loan finance. This might be done by creating a 'public corporation, placed on the same level as the other productive enterprises of the state' that would 'own and administer the state's public buildings, schools, post offices, hospitals. The particular branch of administration has, thus, to pay to this corporation yearly rent for the use of its quarters.... The corporation, in its turn, utilized its rent incomes for paying not only the upkeep of the buildings, but also interest and depreciation on the invested capital.' This proposal had a particularly attractive feature because it meant that 'during a depression we can now expand our construction program for public buildings and finance it out of loans without breaking any budget principles and without endangering the soundness of finances in the long run.'[15]

Myrdal's discourse before the American Economic Association focused on perfecting strategies for future deployment, rather than on a detailed *post-mortem* of the particulars of the Swedish 'experiment.' But it is abundantly clear that much more was going on to lift incomes and employment in the Sweden of the mid-1930s than just the expansionary impact of loan-financed spending on public works. In 1957, Erik Lundberg offered a measured assessment of these events. He then observed,

> The Social Democratic government, which took office in the autumn of 1932, followed an active policy of economic expansion . . . through an increase of government investment and of public works financed by loans. . . . There is no doubt that this new approach had a great and lasting significance in the development of ideas, but the actual measures taken after 1932 were of secondary importance in the revival of 1932–4. The expansionist plans were impeded by such events as the labour dispute in the building industry in 1933–4, and they could not be realized on any large scale until 1934–5, by which time the trade revival was already past its first stage.[16]

Lundberg further maintained that 'in the initial revival of 1932–1934 it also appears that the income-raising effect of exports was of great importance.'[17]

Controversy over temporal priorities once more

It will be recalled from the discussion in the preceding chapter that controversy is still alive over whether members of the Stockholm School or Keynes were first past the post in identifying the crucial ingredients of the 'revolution' that transpired in macro-economics in the 1930s. This polemic had a counterpart in debates over the roles of various contributors in the shaping of expansionary fiscal policies – led by loan-financed public works – to counteract the Great Depression. There was no challenge to the fact that policy-makers in Sweden were well ahead of those elsewhere in implementing such a strategy. Nor did anyone deny that economists in Sweden at that time enjoyed a remarkable degree of access to top officials in government. But a question could still be posed: Was the policy course that the Swedish government had chosen influenced primarily by indigenous economic thinking or by doctrines that had earlier been promulgated abroad?

A doctoral dissertation written by Karl-Gustav Landgren (which appeared in book form in Swedish in 1960) challenged what had been the accepted wisdom on this matter.[18] Landgren correctly identified Ernst Wigforss, the Finance Minister in the Social Democratic government that came to power in 1932, as the moving force behind the adoption of an expansionary fiscal policy. It followed then that the major influences on Wigforss's thinking needed to be tracked. Landgren asserted the arresting finding that Wigforss's thought processes were shaped less by the economists who surrounded him in Stockholm than by his acquaintance with the literature produced by the radical wing of the British Liberal Party, with Keynes in the role of its intellectual leader. The case for large-scale public investment to counter unemployment had been hinted at in the Liberal Party's 'Yellow Book' of 1928 and was spelled out more fully in the pamphlet by Keynes, in collaboration with Hubert Henderson, entitled *Can Lloyd George Do It?* The latter document, published in 1929, called for aggressive spending on public works. Keynesian policy toward the problem of unemployment was thus articulated half a dozen years or so in advance of the theoretical underpinnings supplied with the publication of *The General Theory* in 1936.

Wigforss was certainly familiar with British writings on the case for public works expenditure to stimulate a depressed economy. Though an 'amateur economist,' he was highly respected by the professionals in Stockholm for his familiarity with important contributions to the discipline. Erik Lundberg, for example, remarked that 'on the many occasions in the 1930s when I heard him discuss economic theory with economists, I was impressed by his wide knowledge of economic doctrines.'[19] Myrdal also saluted Wigforss because 'he read the literature more copiously than any of us, he was thoroughly familiar, and in complete sympathy with all the new ideas of the time and took a lively part in discussions between us which run parallel to our various writings.'[20]

But does all this circumstantial evidence add up to a conclusive demonstration that Keynes was the real inspirer of a Swedish fiscal policy committed to deliberate deficits allocated to spending on public works? Some able economists have found this argument to be persuasive. Donald Winch, for example, has argued that 'Wigforss emerges from Landgren's study as the first politician (and socialist?) to grasp the significance of the Keynesian position. It would seem that Keynes should have looked to Stockholm rather than to Roosevelt's Washington for the first practical application of his ideas.'[21] For a time, Mark Blaug was also sympathetic to this position. Writing in 1968, he observed,

> We used to think that the Swedish record of deficit finance was the result of the work of Myrdal and other Swedish economists.... Recent evidence has come to light, however, showing that the Swedish policy of unbalanced budgets to smooth out business cycles was decisively influenced by the writings of the radical wing of the English Liberal Party under Keynes's intellectual leadership....Keynes was a prophet, but not apparently in his own country.[22]

Landgren's thesis was vigorously challenged by Otto Steiger in a dissertation prepared for submission to the University of Uppsala in 1971. (This document was published in a German translation entitled *Studien zur Entstehung der neuen Wirtschaftslehre in Schweden – eine Anti-Kritik* [Studies Concerning the Emergence of the 'New Economics' in Sweden – a Counter-critique].) In Steiger's view, the formulation of Sweden's expansionary fiscal policy in the early 1930s was a distinctly home-grown development. In support of this conclusion, he cited an article published by Wigforss in 1967 in which he described the recovery program as rooted in the 'Social Democratic traditions of thought.'[23] In an essay published in 1960 dealing with the same point, Wigforss acknowledged that he and some of his Social Democratic colleagues had been influenced by the writings of British Fabians and British Liberals (Keynes among them), but that he had not been inspired 'intellectually' by this material. Instead the Swedes had been influenced 'tactically' by observing the programmatic successes and failures of the Fabians and Liberals in Britain. Insights into this experience were held to be helpful in structuring policies in Sweden that would win broad political support.[24] Steiger also undertook a detailed analysis of the timing of Ohlin's various writings on an expansionary public works program to document that the latter's thinking on these matters proceeded independently and anticipated Keynes's recommendations on innovations in fiscal policy.[25]

Some of this disputation comes through as casuistical and uninstructive. Just how important it is to establish definitively the order of temporal priorities on expansionary fiscal policies in the 1930s is less than completely self-evident. The overriding truth about the intellectual environment of the Great Depression was that it stimulated a remarkable degree of resemblance in economic thinking across national boundaries about the search for remedies. Calls for aggressive programs of public works expenditure were then issued in a fair number of countries. This approach to policy was very much 'in the air' in industrialized countries at that time. Such calls were articulated in a variety of languages and emanated from countries identified with quite divergent approaches to economic analysis and policy.

A noteworthy omission

For evidence that counter-cyclical spending on public works was 'in the air' in the inter-war years, one need look no further than the United States. In the context of the post-World War I recession there, serious public discussion of this strategy occurred in the autumn of 1921. Experts were then convened in Washington to advise on the best ways to address that problem, as well as future recurrences of unemployment. The resulting recommendations were published as the report of the 'President's Conference on Unemployment.' The guiding official was not President Harding, however, but his Secretary of Commerce, Herbert Hoover. The Report called for concentrated spending on public works to combat downturns in economic activity and it argued that implementation of that policy would generate a 'multiplying effect of successive use of funds in circulation.' As was the case elsewhere at that time, the absent component in this version of a 'multiplier' concept was the one Kahn supplied in 1931 when demonstrating the limit to successive rounds of expenditure.

As Secretary of Commerce from 1921 to 1928, Hoover commissioned follow-up studies to perfect this strategy. And he also went on record in challenging those who claimed that the 'laws' of the business cycle could not be contained. In his considered view, compensatory spending on public works could successfully counteract downturns in output and employment. As President in 1929 when the crash in the American economy began, Hoover did his best to activate this strategy. Properties of the American federal system, however, limited the amount of direct leverage that he could exert. In ordinary circumstances, the Federal government was responsible for only about ten percent of capital spending in the public sector. In the inter-governmental division of labor, the Federal government's domain was typically restricted to such projects as post offices, Federal court houses, inter-state highways and waterways, and facilities required by the armed forces. The overwhelming bulk of public capital spending – usually some 90 percent of the total – was the responsibility of state and municipal governments. They were expected to take care of the construction needs of the school systems, public hospitals, sewage disposal, city streets, and most of the roads. These units of government were autonomous entities, and Hoover believed that, in the American plan, it was essential that they should remain so.

With the onset of the Depression, Hoover's White House instructed Federal departments and agencies to accelerate spending on useful public works that were already planned. And he appealed to the nation's governors and mayors to step up their spending on projects under their control. In addition, he called upon the big capital spenders in the private sector – for example, railways, electric utilities, telephone, and telegraph – to do likewise in the public interest. In the first year of the Depression, there were some positive responses to Hoover's program. But exhortation was not enough. Meanwhile investment outlays in the bulk of the unregulated business sector as well as in the construction of housing plummeted.[26]

In the considerable discussion of fiscal strategies centered on loan-financed public works in which Swedes and Britons were engaged in the late 1920s and 1930s, American thinking in those years goes unremarked. With respect to the evolution of Myrdal's views on compensatory fiscal strategies, this leaves open an interesting question. He was in the United States in 1929–1930 when Hoover's appeals to state and local governments and to the regulated industries in the private sector were in the headlines. In his *Monetary Equilibrium*, Myrdal mentions in passing the American under-consumptionists,

Foster and Catchings, whose views in favor of an aggressive expansion of public spending as a stabilizer were widely reported.[27] Myrdal was certainly aware of this aspect of policy thinking on the American scene; yet he elected not to speak to it.

Notes

1. G. Myrdal, 'Socialpolitikens dilemma' (The Dilemma of Social Policy), *Spektrum*, 2:4 (1932) 13–31. Translations from the Swedish are by Anna Ankar Barron.
2. Ibid.
3. Ibid.
4. E. Wadensjö, 'The Committee on Unemployment and the Stockholm School,' L. Jonung, ed., *The Stockholm School of Economics Revisited* (Cambridge and New York: Cambridge University Press, 1991), pp. 103–24.
5. R. F. Kahn, 'The Relation of Home Investment to Unemployment,' *Economic Journal*, 41 (June 1931) 173–98.
6. G. Myrdal, *Finanspolitikens ekonomiska verkningar* (*Economic Effecs of Fiscal Policy*), 1934, *passim*. Myrdal's expansionary proposals are also discussed by B. Thomas, *Monetary Policy and Crises: a Study of Swedish Experience* (London: George Routledge and Sons, 1936), and by C. G. Uhr, 'Economists and Policymaking 1930–1936: Sweden's Experience,' *History of Political Economy* (Spring 1977) 102–07.
7. E. Wigforss, 'The Financial Policy during Depression and Boom,' *Annals of the American Academy of Political and Social Science*, 197 (May 1938) 25–39.
8. B. Ohlin, 'Economic Recovery and Labour Market Problems in Sweden: I,' *International Labour Review*, XXXI (April 1935) 507.
9. E. Wigforss, loc. cit., 32.
10. Ibid., 34.
11. G. Möller, 'The Unemployment Policy,' *Annals of the American Academy of Political and Social Science*, 197 (May 1938) 51, 61.
12. E. Wigforss, loc. cit., 37.
13. G. Myrdal, 'Fiscal Policy in the Business Cycle,' *American Economic Review Supplement*, 29 (March 1939) 183.
14. Ibid., 190.
15. Ibid.
16. E. Lundberg, *Business Cycles and Economic Policy* (London: George Allen and Unwin, 1957), p. 54n.
17. Ibid., p. 34.
18. See K.-G. Landgren, *Den 'nya ekonomien' i Sverige: J. M. Keynes, E. Wigforss, B. Ohlin och utvecklingen 1927–1939* (Stockholm: Almquist och Wiksell, 1960). (English translation: The 'New Economics' in Sweden: J. M. Keynes, E. Wigforss, B. Ohlin and Developments, 1927–1939).

19. Lundberg, op. cit., p. 113n.
20. G. Myrdal, *Value in Social Theory*, P. Streeten, ed. (London: Routledge and Kegan Paul, 1958), p. 257n.
21. D. Winch, 'The Keynesian Revolution in Sweden,' *Journal of Political Economy*, 74 (February 1966) 172.
22. M. Blaug, *Economic Theory in Retrospect*, 2nd edition (Cambridge: Cambridge University Press, 1968), p. 663. Blaug backed away from this judgment in the 3rd edition of this work. In the 1978 version, he wrote with reference to the scholarship of Otto Steiger that it 'restores the Swedish schools' claim of originality, and credits them with having a decisive influence on Swedish economic policy well before 1936.' See Blaug, op. cit., 3rd edition, 1978, p. 695.
23. As quoted by C. G. Uhr, 'The Emergence of the "New Economics" in Sweden: a Review of a Study by Otto Steiger,' *History of Political Economy*, 5 (Spring 1973) 259.
24. Ibid., 248–49.
25. O. Steiger, 'Bertil Ohlin and the Origins of the Keynesian Revolution,' *History of Political Economy*, 8 (Fall 1976) 341–66.
26. For additional detail on Hoover's strategy of counter-cyclical public works spending and the attempt to implement it, see W. J. Barber, *From New Era to New Deal: Herbert Hoover, the Economists, and American Economic Policy, 1921–33* (New York and Cambridge: Cambridge University Press, 1985).
27. G. Myrdal, *Monetary Equilibrium* (London: W. Hodge and Company, 1939), p. 8.

5
The Population Question and Swedish Social Policy in the 1930s

In 1933, Myrdal was named the Lars Hierta Professor of Economics and Public Finance in the University of Stockholm. Cassel was delighted with this appointment. Even though he regarded Myrdal as 'the most dangerous man in Sweden' on account of his political views, Cassel still announced that he was proud to have him as his successor.[1]

Reports on fiscal policies for the Ministry of Finance, as we have seen, engaged part of Myrdal's writing time in 1933–1934, but no means the whole of it. In company with Alva, he was also at work on a book entitled *Kris i befolkningsfrågan* (Crisis in the Population Question). This was very much a collaborative effort and it ignited a firestorm of controversy unlike anything either Myrdal had yet experienced. In the early 1930s, a number of influential segments of Swedish society were discomfited in the extreme by candid public discourse on sexual matters. Indeed a statute – dating from 1910 – was still on the books that declared it unlawful to promote or to disseminate information about contraception. There must also have been a fair amount of tongue-wagging in the senior ranks of the University of Stockholm's economics faculty. When the book appeared in late 1934, Cassel denounced it in the popular press. Heckscher was bitterly outraged, suggesting that Gunnar's talents were temperamentally better suited to those of a 'full-time agitator' than to a career of dispassionate scholarship.[2] There were some arresting linguistic innovations as well. The love seats in the University's common rooms were dubbed 'Myrdal couches' and the infinitive 'to Myrdal' was taken to mean 'to engage in sexual intercourse.'

The Myrdals' written contribution to public debate on population questions appeared in three iterations. The first was the 1934 book on the population 'crisis.' The second took the form of Reports issued by the Royal Commission on Population, organized in response to the excitement the book had generated. Gunnar served as a member of this Commission, with Alva as a consultant and member of one of its subcommittees. Its reports, published in 17 official documents between 1936 and 1938, elaborated and substantiated the treatment the Myrdals had given to this topic in 1934. Finally, in 1938, Gunnar was invited to deliver the prestigious Godkin Lectures at Harvard University, which he entitled *Population: A Problem for Democracy.*[3] (The Godkin Lectures, established in 1903, were created to bring an outstanding public figure to the University to speak to 'the essentials of free government and the duties of the citizen.') Myrdal's lectures were published in 1940 by the Harvard University Press. This statement represents the mature form of the couple's thinking on these matters.

The core argument of the Godkin Lectures

Myrdal began by reminding his listeners that issues of population had occupied a central position in the development of classical political economy. Latterly, however, this subject matter had engaged the attention of very few economists. This was unfortunate. It was now time to move population study out of the shadows and into the spotlight.

He proposed to address this theme by using Sweden as a laboratory for the study of population dynamics. He acknowledged that his own country's experience could not be regarded as representative. Nevertheless, its history lent itself usefully for purposes of a case study for a number of reasons. In the first instance, the country's racial homogeneity was a recommendation. This meant that population developments there were not contaminated by pro-natalist strivings of competing ethnic groups. Secondly, the country had no imperialistic ambitions and was thus spared from patriotic propaganda that had been known to influence population size elsewhere. In addition, Sweden, in its recent history, had been recognized for its record of peaceful political stability. Unlike the belligerents in World War I, it had no 'lost generation.'

Tracing Swedish population dynamics over the past three-quarters of a century or so was especially instructive in light of the fundamental structural transformation in the nation's economy during that period. In the 1870s, roughly 75 percent of the population was engaged in agriculture. By the mid-1930s, by contrast, only about one-third of the population was still on the farm. Meanwhile, industrialization and urbanization had been accompanied by a major reduction in the birth rate. The reasons for this phenomenon were not difficult to comprehend. There was a sharp distinction between the economics of family size in rural and urban settings. On the farm, children could properly be seen as economic assets: even from fairly young ages, they could perform chores that contributed positively to the output of the family enterprise. In urban areas, the situation was the reverse. Children there tended to be economic liabilities who represented net drains on the family's resources. Another factor also contributed to the rural–urban differentials. Knowledge of and access to contraceptives was much easier in the cities than on the farms.

Indications of an impending population 'crisis' began to surface in the mid-1920s when the net reproduction rate fell below the magnitude necessary to sustain the country's population size. Nearly a decade later – when the Myrdals were producing their diagnosis of the situation – this matter had taken on still greater urgency. The net reproductive rate had fallen to about 75 percent of the level needed for population replacement. This state of affairs presented a real and present danger that threatened the continuation of the nation and its culture.

Why had the citizenry failed to perceive the dimensions of this problem? Myrdal's discussion of this point turned on a distinction between two sets of attitudes. First, a conservative one that supported the suppression of contraception with the expectation that this would insure adequacy in population size. A second entertained much more radical views – and ones that had been influenced by neo-Malthusian doctrines. From this perspective, contraception should be welcomed and encouraged: an absolute reduction in population size could be viewed as a positive economic good. Sooner or later, Myrdal argued, the mismatch between public perceptions and the existential reality would provoke an 'ideological crisis.' Such a crisis, he maintained, had occurred in Sweden in the autumn of 1934. He explained it as follows:

> The spark which touched off the 1934 fireworks was a book which, though a rather heavy sociological treatise of four hundred pages, was very widely circulated in all social classes. The population situation immediately began to be discussed intensively in the press and on the radio; a flood of pamphlets appeared, and the subject was shortly brought to the floor of Parliament and debated by all political parties. A Royal Commission on the Swedish population problem was set to work in the spring of 1935.

The book in question here was, of course, the Myrdals' *Kris i befolkningsfrågan*. Neither the book's title nor its authors were identified in the published version of the Godkin Lectures.[4]

While Myrdal attached high importance to the threat to national survival posed by recent population trends, he advanced other reasons as well to support programs aimed to sustain a constant population size. (Throughout the discussion, it was presupposed that a growing population was not a feasible target in Swedish conditions.) In his view, blocking a reduction in population size was an imperative for healthy and sustained prosperity. The central argument here was of a piece with his thinking about fiscal measures to stabilize the macro-economy. It appeared to be self-evident that a shrinking population would be a deterrent to generating investment spending sufficient to offset the community's saving and to avoid economic stagnation. Capital spending in certain sectors was especially sensitive to rates of decline in population size. Outlays for housing – a major component of aggregate capital spending – would obviously be dampened. Similarly, requirements for investment spending on infrastructure in both the private and the public sectors would be diminished. Myrdal summarized the situation as follows: 'A declining population will increase investment risks all round and, even apart from that, will lessen the demand for new investment. Since in an aging society monetary savings are kept up, the result will be a continuous tendency toward investment falling short of saving.' From his writings on compensatory fiscal policies, he was well aware that governmental intervention as a spender could be introduced to address this shortfall. But this activity, he maintained, would be 'a difficult task, if [government] is not to replace private enterprise over the whole field.'[5]

Myrdal regarded the prospect of such an outcome as distressing in the extreme. And he spoke to it at some length. The type of Socialism that could be expected to develop in circumstances of population decline would be 'a peculiar brand' that would 'take on an administrative, bureaucratic, senile character; it will be the bureaucratic administration of the liquidation of a people. Much less takes care of itself in a declining economy than in one that is growing; the bureaucratic apparatus must therefore increase. This apparatus becomes less dynamic, less effective, not only because it comes to rest principally in the power of old men, but also because of a heretofore unmentioned reason: the best, the most dynamic intelligences cannot come to feel a very great interest in the administration of a liquidation. Even one who was a Socialist in politics, but who has felt the pulse of progress in his veins, who has loved free initiative and advance, must feel cheerless before these prospects. He hardly expected this to be the outlook for Socialism. He would even be tempted to defend private capitalism if by that means he could revivify dynamic progress.'[6]

But this was not all. A society undergoing population decline would be unattractive for yet another reason. Conditions of economic stagnation were not calculated to produce career opportunities that the young potential entrants to the labor force were entitled to. Another strain on the cohesiveness of the body politic could thus be expected.

Possible policy responses

Relative to dictatorships, Myrdal suspected that democracies were at a disadvantage in formulating and executing a rational population policy. 'Imperialistic nationalism,' he wrote, 'is naturally ready to accept and preach the value of quantity of population, but an aggressive expansionist policy is the very denial of democracy, since the principle both of a ruling class and a ruling nation means oligarchy.' As he saw it, the 'political basis for a population policy was weaker in democracies' for an additional reason: '. . . in the ideological basis of democratic society it is deeply inherent that the people are sovereign, that the private individual and his aims have a primacy over the state and its strivings . . . .'[7]

Whatever the obstacles to a rational population policy might be, both Myrdals were convinced that the stakes were so high that maximum effort should be applied to overcome them. Their 1934 book proposed a strategy for such a policy which was absorbed into the thinking of the Royal Commission on Population. Its essential features were also described in the Godkin Lectures.

There was no ambiguity about the objective to be sought: the achievement of a population of constant size. It was fully appreciated that the realization of this goal would be difficult. This was apparent when the dimensions of the task were calculated: given the fact that a proportion of marriages would be sterile, the fertile marriages would need to produce four children. This would clearly require a significant acceleration in Sweden's birth rate, which was then the lowest in Europe.

The centerpiece of this strategy was state intervention that would tend to equalize consumption across social classes and income groups. Put slightly differently, the program's aim would be to eliminate – through governmental action – the incremental expense burdens associated with childbearing and child-rearing by poorer families. Specific proposals were introduced, for example, to upgrade housing conditions through the provision of public housing and subsidies to rentals in the private sector. Nutritional standards would be elevated through direct distribution of healthy foodstuffs to families. (In the economic environment of Sweden in the mid-1930s, it was anticipated that such supplies could be made available through surpluses that had arisen as by-products of governmental price supports introduced to bolster a distressed farming sector.) In short, this action was thought of as a form of 'domestic dumping.' Publicly funded health services would be made available to all, and substantial maternity benefits would be paid to cover costs incurred by childbirth. Another innovative suggestion was the institution of 'marriage loans' to assist young couples in setting up a household at an earlier age than would otherwise have been possible. Primary and secondary education was already funded by public bodies. A system of state scholarships was to be added to the mix to support students from poorer families who needed help if they pursued higher education.

What this all amounted to was the agenda for the Swedish welfare state, vintage mid-1930s.

Implementing the policy agenda

In 1936, Myrdal was elected to the Swedish Senate as the representative for Dalarna. He thus had been thrust into the realities of hands-on practical politics. Self-evidently, he was keen to push the recommendations that he and Alva had advanced in the 1934 book which, in turn, had been endorsed by the Royal Commission on Population.

But there was a formidable obstacle confronting Parliamentary adoption of this legislative program. The transfer of benefits to the lower income groups called for in this vision of a welfare state would be expensive. The bulk of that burden would necessarily be borne by conservative factions in the community who could be expected to mount considerable opposition. There was more than a touch of ingenuity in the political maneuvering that neutralized potential opponents. The appeal to the conservatives – whose views were at odds with those of the sponsors of the legislative program – was presented within the following framework. The state interventions called for, it was argued, were designed to ward off the curse of population decline with all of its attendant social and economic hazards. Conservatives thus needed to be educated on the vital importance of sacrificing their private economic interests in favor of a higher good – namely national survival itself. Myrdal acknowledged that this tactic played to attitudes of patriotic nationalism – not normally an attribute high in his rank order of virtues – but he regarded it as justifiable in the circumstances and 'mild' in form. He offered the following overall assessment:

> In a general way, it can be ascertained that that actualization of the population problem turns political opinions away from conservatism and toward radicalism. This is true as far as issues of economic, distributional, and social policy are concerned. The population problem is utilized, as the conservative Swedish economist bitterly complains, as a 'crow-bar for social reforms.'[8]

Myrdal elaborated on this point by drawing attention to attitudes of the typical conservative citizen 'with an honest and deep-rooted interest in family and nation' – who would 'often find it even disgusting that the [population] problem... would now suddenly turn into a most dangerous weapon in the hands of his adversaries, gaining support for a remolding of society in a direction contrary to all conservative principles.... It even happens that former conservatives, preponderantly intellectuals and experts such as preachers, teachers, doctors, etc., because of their interest in certain aspects of the practical population problem, turn to thorough-going radicalism in social policy more generally. The aggregate result, in any case, is that, although as usual in a democracy all actual reform questions are hotly debated, the very frontier of political discussion and action has moved several miles towards the left.'[9]

The bulk of the recommended legislative program was enacted in the 1937 session of the Swedish Parliament which became popularly identified as the 'mothers and babies' session. Most of the proposed benefits were approved with but minor modifications. A sweeping program of highly progressive taxation was also enacted. In addition, the 1910 statute outlawing discussions of contraception was struck down and discriminations against pregnant women in the labor force were banned.[10]

The architecture of the Swedish welfare state was thus put in place under the smokescreen of the population argument. The radical measures taken were not justified on grounds that they were desirable *per se*. The rationale offered rested instead on the claim that they were essential to protecting the national interest from the hazards associated with population shrinkage.

The dark side of a rational population policy

The formulation of a rational population policy compatible with the principles of democracy was a matter of pride for Myrdal. He was at pains to distinguish this conception from population policies promulgated in totalitarian countries. The latter were motivated by patriotic urgings to 'stimulate' the breeding of children. The democratic version, on the other hand, was based on providing a catalyst to voluntary parental choice to follow 'their natural urge to marry and to have children' that would remove the economic obstacles to family-building. Thanks to this intervention by the state, a positive quantitative response to family enlargement could be expected. But no less important was improvement in the quality of the population. This would follow from the package of benefits provided by the state. Growth in quantity and increased quality could be expected to go hand-in-hand.[11]

In the Swedish case, all of this had been premised on the need to increase the number of 'desired' children, but also to reduce the number of 'undesired' births. This was the basis for universalizing knowledge of and access to modern techniques of birth control. Parents could thus plan systematically on family size, and the number of unintended pregnancies – whether within marriage or outside it – would fall. But a question remained about the treatment of 'undesirable' births.

Swedish policy on this point was at odds with the principle of voluntary decision-making with regard to procreation. A law enacted in May 1934 mandated compulsory sterilization of persons deemed incapable of consent – that is, the insane and imbecile. The Royal Commission on Population further recommended recognition of a right to voluntary sterilization in such cases as hereditary insanity, nervous or physical disease, imbecility, deformity, epilepsy, and so on. By 1939, however, there was no Parliamentary action on such an extension of sterilization.[12]

Widespread awareness of Nazi practices in the 1930s and 1940s in the name of 'racial purification' have generally discredited policies identified with arguments based on eugenics. To put this matter in perspective, it must be recalled that eugenics in the inter-war years was touted by liberal opinion in various parts of the world as key to improvement in the human condition. In the United States, for example, Irving Fisher of Yale University – widely regarded as the greatest scientific economist that America had as yet produced and a tireless champion of social causes – regarded eugenics to be worth crusading for. In his judgment, it was of paramount importance to alert people in power to 'what eugenics means.' And he added,

> this could be done quietly and simply without violence to existing ideas of what is right and proper. It could be done by segregation of the sexes for defectives, feeble-minded, idiots, epileptics, insane,

> etc. By this kind of isolation, we can save the blood stream of our race from a tremendous amount of contamination. Sterilization is also a means which may be advantageously applied in extreme cases.[13]

A number of the progressive and respectable philanthropies of the day – for example, Harriman and Carnegie money – provided generous support to this cause. What happened in Sweden in the way the topic of eugenics played out in the 1930s was not an isolated case.

Some parallels

Just as members of the Stockholm School and the emerging Keynesians in Britain were thinking along similar lines about macroeconomic theory and policy in the mid-1930s, so also was there some convergence in thought about the economic implications of declining population growth. We have seen how Myrdal formulated the issue when addressing conditions in Sweden. Prior to the Godkin Lectures in May 1938, his analytic treatment of this problem was little known – if at all – outside Scandinavia. It should be noted that Denmark and Finland, inspired by the Swedish example, created Population Commissions of their own.

Keynes's contribution to the discussion received much wider attention. He spoke to this matter in an essay entitled 'Some Economic Consequences of Declining Population Growth,' published in the *Eugenics Review* in April 1937. It came naturally for him to explore the implications of this phenomenon within the new analytic framework that he had constructed. Thus, he directed attention to the impact of declining population growth rates on the propensity to consume and on the inducement to invest. His findings demonstrated that population trends could be expected to influence both of these components of aggregate demand negatively, an unfortunate outcome from the point of view of achieving and sustaining full employment.

Keynes's discussion of this subject had an important ramification in the United States. Harvard's Alvin H. Hansen – who came to be known as the leading apostle of Keynesianism in the United States – gave close attention to its argument. He had initially reviewed

The General Theory unsympathetically, concluding that 'the book under review is not a landmark in the sense that it lays a foundation for a new economics....The book is more a symptom of economic trends than a foundation stone on which a science can be built.'[14] Hansen's attention to Keynes's writing on declining population growth proved to be a crucial part of his conversion experience to the new analytic perspective. Keynes's interpretation seemed to mesh well with the essential facts of American economic history over the past three-quarters of a century or so. In the late nineteenth and early twentieth centuries, the country's capacity to absorb capital had appeared to be virtually unlimited: investment opportunities were then abundant and called for major allocations of resources to tame the continent and to meet the needs of a rapidly expanding population. In such an environment, economic expansion had been easy to achieve. In marked contrast was the nation's situation in the 1930s. The Western frontier had been closed and population growth rates were declining. Hansen connected all the dots in his presidential address to the American Economic Association in December 1938, in which he presented a full-blown statement of the 'stagnation thesis' and employed the Keynesian analytic categories when doing so. The central problem, as he then diagnosed it, was to generate a 'volume of investment expenditures adequate for that level of income which could be achieved were all factors employed.' Reaching this goal, however, was increasingly difficult because the long-term determinants of economic activity were weighted on the side of stagnation, not growth. It was thus the task of economic policy to enlarge aggregate demand through measures designed to increase the propensity to consume and through an expanded program of public expenditures. The alternative was a future of 'sick recoveries which die in their infancy and depressions which feed on themselves and leave a hard and seemingly immovable core of unemployment.'[15]

Notes

1. W. A. Jackson, *Gunnar Myrdal and America's Conscience* (Chapel Hill: University of North Carolina Press, 1990), p. 75.
2. S. Bok, *Alva Myrdal: A Daughter's Memoir* (Reading, MA: Addison-Wesley Publishing Company, 1991), p. 15.

3. G. Myrdal, *Population: A Problem for Democracy* (Cambridge, MA: Harvard University Press, 1940), p. 76.
4. In an article published in the *Annals of the American Academy of Political and Social Science*, Myrdal described this crisis in much the same words and did identify the authors and title. See Myrdal, 'Population Problems and Policies,' 197 (May 1938), p. 202 of that journal.
5. G. Myrdal, *Population: A Problem for Democracy*, p. 164.
6. Ibid., pp. 165–66.
7. Ibid., p. 34.
8. Ibid., p. 96.
9. Ibid., pp. 96–97.
10. A full inventory of legislative enactments in this period can be found in A. Myrdal, 'A Programme for Family Security in Sweden,' *International Labour Review*, 39 (June 1939) 723–63.
11. G. Myrdal, *Population* . . . , pp. 202–05.
12. A. Myrdal, loc. cit., p. 740.
13. I. Fisher, *The Works of Irving Fisher: A Crusader for Social Causes*, Volume 13, W. J. Barber, ed. (London: Pickering and Chatto, 1997), p. 170.
14. A. H. Hansen, 'Mr. Keynes on Underemployment Equilibrium,' *Journal of Political Economy*, 44 (October 1936) 686.
15. A. H. Hansen, 'Economic Progress and Declining Population Growth,' *American Economic Review*, 29 (March 1939) 5. For a fuller discussion of the background of this episode, see W. J. Barber, 'The Career of Alvin H. Hansen in the 1920s and 1930s: a Study in Intellectual Transformation,' *History of Political Economy*, 19 (Summer 1987) 191–205.

6
An American Dilemma: The Negro Problem and Modern Democracy (1944)

Over Myrdal's long and multifaceted career, the preparation of *An American Dilemma: The Negro Problem and Modern Democracy* stands out as a signal event. In the United States particularly, those who may be totally ignorant of his fundamental achievements in economics are likely still to identify him with this book. It was massive in scale: just under 1500 pages in all (including 10 appendices). The outlays needed to complete it were record-shattering for a body of research in the social sciences – some $300 000 in 1930s dollars (or roughly ten times that sum if measured in dollars of the early twenty-first century). And the work had impact. It can properly be regarded as one of the few works of scholarship to alter the course of history.[1] Even so, at a point or two along the way, it was touch-and-go whether or not this project would be brought to fruition.

The background

The inspiration for this study can be tracked to officials in the Carnegie Corporation, a foundation established in 1911 by a steel magnate of the robber-baronial era, Andrew Carnegie, who believed it was sinful to die rich. The philanthropy was charged to 'promote advancement and diffusion of knowledge,' a charge that could be interpreted with some degree of elasticity. Most Americans in the early decades of the twentieth century probably associated Carnegie's generosity with subsidies to public libraries throughout the country. The Corporation was active in a number of fields, including grant-making on behalf of the Negro population in the United States and of the indigenous peoples of Africa. It had, for example, regularly provided funds to educational institutions serving Negroes in the American South. In addition, it had underwritten the massive *African Survey* prepared by Lord Hailey, a retired senior administrator in British India, that was published in 1938, as well as a study of the circumstances of 'Poor Whites' in the Union of South Africa that appeared in the early 1930s. But, by the later 1930s, there was uncertainty among senior officials about the priorities the Corporation should establish to guide future grant-making to improve race relations in the United States.

A need for expert guidance on this matter was first expressed in 1937 by Newton D. Baker, an independent-minded Trustee of the Carnegie Corporation, who had served variously as President Woodrow Wilson's Secretary of War during World War I and previously as Mayor of Cleveland, Ohio. In some respects, Baker was an unlikely advocate for programs designed to enhance the welfare of America's Negroes. A son of a Confederate cavalry officer in the Civil War, he had grown up in the South and his thinking on racial matters still bore some of the markings of racial attitudes then characteristic of that region. But his experience as a public official had also taught him that the country faced potentially explosive racial problems and that these problems had been exacerbated by the Great Depression and the accelerated migration of Negroes from the rural South to the urban North. On his initiative, the Carnegie Corporation determined that it was timely to commission an expert study to inform its decision-making with regard to grants in this sensitive area. And this was very much a live issue. Professional educators were divided in their views. One school, influenced by the thinking of Booker T. Washington (founder of the Tuskegee Institute), held that the education of Negroes should focus on the vocational and the practical and that no training should be provided for jobs that the Southern establishment would bar them from filling. On the other hand, followers of W. E. B. Du Bois – the first Negro to be awarded a Harvard doctorate – maintained that Negroes should enjoy the same educational opportunities as whites.

Who, then, should be recruited for this assignment? In the early going, it was decided to rule out American scholars. This could be justified on grounds that Americans might be perceived – whether rightly or wrongly – as lacking a sufficient detachment. (This decision also meant that controversy over whether the principal investigator should be black or white could be finessed.) The Trustees gave serious consideration to two foreigners steeped in experience in colonial matters: Britain's Lord Hailey, who had directed the acclaimed *African Survey*, and Hendrik Mouw, a highly reputed colonial administrator in the Dutch East Indies. The name of Roy Harrod, an economist at Christ Church, Oxford, was also mentioned, but it appears not to have been strongly in the running. Americans consulted by the Carnegie Corporation took strong exception to the appointment of a national from any country with an imperial legacy. Head-hunting then shifted to Scandinavia and Switzerland.

In this context, Myrdal's name came to the fore. He lacked first-hand exposure to racial problems, but this very innocence could be regarded as a recommendation. He obviously had left a major mark on economics in Sweden at a prodigiously young age and his credentials as a scholar whose writings displayed impressive range and depth were impeccable. As an elected member of the Swedish Parliament, he could bring experience in practical politics to the assignment. His considerable reputation as a leading architect of Sweden's welfare state also counted in his favor. Not least, his year as a Rockefeller Foundation Fellow in 1929–1930 had acquainted him with important aspects of American society.

Myrdal's name was placed in nomination by Beardsley Ruml, sometime Dean of the Social Sciences at the University of Chicago, who had met Myrdal during his sojourn as a Rockefeller Fellow. By 1937, Ruml had left academic life in favor of a senior appointment in the business community, but he pursued an active avocation as a talent scout for various New Deal agencies and for foundations. Ruml's opinion carried clout. His advocacy of Myrdal was endorsement enough to convince Frederick P. Keppel, President of the Carnegie Corporation, to proceed with an appointment. In the late summer of 1937, Keppel proposed to Myrdal that he become the Director of 'a comprehensive study of the Negro in the United States, to be undertaken in a wholly objective and dispassionate way as a social phenomenon.... Our idea, so far as we have developed it, would be to invite one man to be responsible for the study as a whole, but to place at his disposal the services of a group of associates, Americans, who would be competent to deal as experts with the anthropological, economic, educational and social aspects of the question, including public health and public administration.'[2]

In light of the way this story unfolded, it is noteworthy that Myrdal turned down this initial invitation. When it was extended, he apparently believed that an acceptance would compromise his ambitions in Swedish politics. By the Spring of 1938 – and after a Ruml visit to Stockholm – he underwent a change of heart. He then agreed to direct the study and arrived in the United States in early September 1938 to begin the work.

The preparation: Phase I

At Keppel's suggestion, Myrdal began with an extended tour of the American South. He was accompanied by Richard Sterner, a Swedish statistician (who was to be a fixture in this enterprise from beginning to end), and by Jackson Davis, a liberally minded white Southerner. The expedition was much more than a tour of town halls and county seats. As Myrdal put it, 'We established contact with a great number of white and Negro leaders in various activities; visited universities, colleges, churches, and various state and community agencies as well as factories and plantations; talked to police officers, teachers, preachers, politicians, journalists, agriculturalists, workers, sharecroppers, and in fact, all sorts of people, colored and white. . . .'[3] Negro-owned funeral parlors proved to be especially useful places for conversations. In this line of business, Negroes enjoyed a monopoly without fear of competition from Southern whites. Moreover, what took place in these premises was beyond the purview of the Southern establishment.

Myrdal was shocked by what he saw in the 'Jim Crow' world of the American South and returned to the Carnegie Corporation's headquarters in New York with a sobered understanding of the dimensions of the problem he had undertaken to analyze.

He wrote to Keppel proposing that the Corporation form a committee composed of a Southern white, a Northern white, and a Negro to work with him in preparing the final report. Keppel would have none of it: the work product should bear the stamp of a single individual without the shelter of blurred responsibilities in a document produced by a committee. This did not mean that the Director of the study would be denied expert help that he felt in need of. A core staff was engaged that included Richard Sterner; Ralph J. Bunche, a Negro political scientist at Howard University with a Harvard Ph.D.; Guy B. Johnson, a white sociologist based at the University of North Carolina; Paul H. Norgren, a Harvard-trained economist; and Doxey Wilkerson, a Negro professor of sociology at Howard University.[4] This group commissioned background monographs from members of the first team in American social sciences – both white and black – with demonstrated credentials in the study of race relations. The scope of the enterprise was staggering – topics included tests of Negro intelligence, mental disease among Negroes, miscegenation, Negro churches and associations, the health of the Negro, the Negro family, the Negro and crime, the Negro press, recreation and amusement among American Negroes, Negro population movements, the Negro in the American economic system, the Negro in American education, the bases of social stratification in Negro society, and so on. Altogether, some 15,000 typescript pages were submitted in this phase of the proceedings. A number of these monographs were published as free-standing volumes.[5] Among his assistants, Myrdal formed a particularly close bond with Bunche. The two of them traveled together on a fact-finding tour of the South which included some hair-raising moments when in the company of segregationists. For his part, Bunche admired Myrdal, even though he referred to his boss as a 'Swedish Simon Legree' because of the demanding pace of his work schedule.[6]

The commissioned studies cut a wide swath through the considerable range of topics investigated. At this stage, however, Myrdal was not satisfied that an overarching theme had yet emerged to shape the organization of the final study. There was, nevertheless, a near consensus among contributors that the fundamental factor controlling the plight of the Negro masses was their miserable economic condition. This suggested that there was little hope for substantial improvement in the absence of a transformation in the economic status of this segment of the population. Meanwhile, the prospects that such a transformation could be accomplished were dimmed by the handicaps imposed by a discriminatory economic and political system. Removing those barriers to advancement, however, was hardly thinkable without a major change in the American polity. In the atmosphere of 1940, that seemed unlikely.

The German invasion of Denmark and Norway in the Spring of 1940 produced an unanticipated interruption in the Carnegie Corporation study. Both Gunnar Myrdal and his wife Alva believed that their place was properly in Sweden during this time of stress (when there appeared to be solid ground for thinking that their home country would be the next target of Nazi territorial aspirations). Frederick Keppel concurred. Samuel A. Stouffer was deputized as acting director in Myrdal's absence. The issue of whether or not the undertaking would ever be completed was then very much in doubt.

A productive Swedish interlude

Upon their return to Sweden, the Myrdals found their home country to be suffering from very badly bruised morale. To be sure, Sweden had managed to avoid belligerency – as well as the status of an occupied country – but it had done so at considerable psychic cost. Its government had yielded to the demands of the Nazi war machine by allowing the German military to cross Swedish soil en route to Norway. Though no one claimed that resistance by the Swedish army would have changed the outcome, Sweden's complicity in the invasion and occupation of a friendly neighbor was certainly less than honorable. In the view of the Myrdals, their homeland seemed to have lost its bearings. Freedoms of speech and expression were curtailed out of fear that overt criticism of the Nazi regime would provoke a German attack. Something precious about the traditional civil liberties of Swedes had been compromised, if not altogether lost. Jointly, the Myrdals chose to address such concerns with their pens. The result was a book entitled *Kontakt med Amerika* ('Contact with America') that became a best seller in Sweden in 1941.

Whatever its imperfections, America, they argued, had developed a 'creed' that spoke to the integrity of enlightened political values. This was evidenced in conversations in the United States with both the intelligentsia and rank-and-file citizens of all skin colorations. The creed's substance was embodied in the language of the Declaration of Independence and the Constitution with affirmations of liberty and justice for all and that 'all men are created equal.' The Myrdals acknowledged that the reality of American life – especially in race relations – did not measure up to that ideal. Nevertheless, their contacts with Americans in all walks of life convinced them of the vital significance of this 'creed.' Reverence for it was virtually universal. Even Southern racists paid homage, however contradictory their behavior might be. 'In our view,' they wrote, ' "American ideals" form the cement, the unifying force in this continental democracy.'[7]

Addressing specifically the issue of race relations, they wrote,

> The Negro problem, just like all other difficult social problems, is... first and foremost a problem in the Americans' own heart. One can also say that it represents a conflict between a national ideology... and various local ideologies which diverge from it. Both kinds are contained within the same American, and their conflict within him reflects the nation's perpetual ongoing moral and social development.[8]

These words were written in the context of a document directed to a Sweden then Nazi-circumscribed. But they also helped to shape a major conceptual clarification that would subsequently become central to the structure of the Carnegie Corporation study.

Elaborating on this theme, the Myrdals insisted that 'moral ideas really represent social forces, although unfortunately not the only ones and not always the strongest.' And they chided American social scientists for downplaying the force of moral ideals. This situation, Myrdal maintained, could be explained as follows: 'In America, a rather extreme materialistic view of history has become dominant within social science, especially sociology, in the last generation. For our part, we consider this tendency to be the most questionable one-sidedness within an otherwise especially differentiated and excellent social research. It originated as a basically moral reaction against an earlier generation's one-sided idealism. Sociology developed in America as the writings of ministers and social reformers. It broke free, especially under Sumner and the Chicago School through studying with the utmost suspicion all the arguments containing morality.'[9] This line of thought would be echoed in the ultimate version of the Carnegie Corporation project.

Walter A. Jackson has well summarized the intended purpose of *Kontakt med Amerika*:

> *Kontakt* was a resistance book designed to convince Swedish readers that the triumph of Hitler's vaunted New Order of

> Europe was not inevitable. The United States, which had not then entered the war, was portrayed as a source of hope for occupied Europe. . . . They sought to make the Swedish people more conscious of their democratic traditions as a counterforce to defeatism and acquiescence in the inevitability of a Nazi-dominated Europe.[10]

But, as Jackson further noted, *Kontakt med Amerika* also served an additional purpose. It generated formulations that were to shape the conceptual architecture of the study of America's Negro problem.

Drafting the final text

When the expected German occupation of Sweden did not materialize, Myrdal decided to return to the United States in March 1941 to resume work on the Carnegie Corporation study. He was again joined by Richard Sterner, the statistician he had brought with him from Sweden in 1938, who had been anchored to the project from the start. Soon thereafter, Arnold Rose, a talented graduate student in sociology from the University of Chicago, rounded out a triumvirate that would see the study through to completion. The final stages of the drafting process occurred at Dartmouth College and at Princeton University.

The unifying vision, lacking at the end of the first phase, was now in place. The central theme was signaled in the title: *An American Dilemma: The Negro Problem and American Democracy.* This choice of words encapsulated the fundamental problem – the disjunction between the ideals of the 'American creed' and the observable social reality. And there could be no mistaking that this was a distinctively American problem. An analogous line of argument, for example, could certainly not have been fitted to the discussion of racial discriminations in South Africa during the supremacy of its Nationalist Party from the 1950s through the 1980s. In the years of high apartheid, there was no conflict between the official orthodoxy and reigning social practices.

The insights into American race relations that Myrdal articulated in *Kontakt med Amerika* struck a refreshingly novel chord. There was a link between his characterization of the nature of America's 'dilemma' and a formulation he had offered in 1932 when diagnosing the condition of Sweden's Social Democratic Party. He then spoke to the 'dilemma' Sweden faced during the depression and described it as a 'moral issue.' (In this instance, the dilemma referred to the challenge of melding social welfare programs associated with classical liberalism with interventionist policies required in the 1930s.) There is a striking parallelism between that train of thought and the title given to the opening section of *An American Dilemma*: 'The Negro Problem as a Moral Issue.'

The reader of *An American Dilemma* could be left in no doubt about the book's central messages – they were italicized in the text. In the introduction, Myrdal wrote,

> *The American Negro problem is a problem in the heart of the American... The 'American Dilemma,' referred to in the title of this book, is the ever-raging conflict between, on the one hand, the valuations preserved on the general plane which we shall call 'the American Creed,' where the American thinks, talks, and acts under the influence of his national and Christian precepts, and, on the other hand, the valuations on specific planes of individual and group living, where personal and local interests; economic, social, and sexual jealousies; considerations of community prestige and conformity; group prejudice against particular persons or types of people; and all sorts of miscellaneous wants, impulses, and habits dominate his outlook.*[11]

An internal dynamic was built into this situation: tension between the ideal and the real would itself be an agent for change. This line of argument reinforced the conclusion, stated in italics, in the 'Author's Preface': *'Not since Reconstruction has there been more reason to anticipate fundamental changes in American race relations, changes which will involve a development toward American ideals.'*[12] In the America of the early 1940s – which was marked by ugly race riots in Northern cities – this projection of the future course of events was bold indeed. And it ran counter to the thinking of most of the recognized experts on American race relations.

Myrdal's prognosis was influenced in no small measure by the intellectual style he had developed in his prior work in economics. Methodological appendices in *An American Dilemma* spelled out the connections. Valuations and their impact on social research and social behavior had been his persisting intellectual preoccupation. He had addressed aspects of these issues in *The Political Element in the Development of Economic Theory* in 1931. He had then argued that a *wert-frei* economics could be achieved if it were purged of the metaphysical baggage inherent in mainstream economic theorizing. When he returned to this theme in *An American Dilemma*, there was a difference. He was then persuaded that value judgments were inescapable in the conduct of social research. The researcher, however, was under an obligation to state explicitly the valuations that informed his work. But that was not all. The conscientious scholar was not at liberty to select guiding valuations arbitrarily. Myrdal insisted that *'the value premises should be selected by the criterion of relevance and significance to the culture under study.'*[13] For the purposes of his study of the Negro problem, he regarded the valuations appropriate to the shaping of its structure as virtually self-evident. They were the ideals of the 'American creed.' He was convinced that there could be no challenging their goodness of 'fit' to American social reality.

The message of *An American Dilemma* was influenced as well by a principle of 'cumulative causation,' a notion Myrdal had absorbed from Wicksell which he had utilized to good effect in his own *Monetary Equilibrium*, published in its first iteration in 1932. The crucial issue here – contrary to the teaching of mainstream neoclassical economics – was that a disturbance to an initial state of equilibrium could not be expected to stimulate compensating reactions tending to restore that equilibrium. Instead the disturbance might well breed changes that would move the system still further away from the original position. When adapting this conception to the study of American race relations, Myrdal argued as follows, 'We assume the "plane of living" of the Negroes to be considerably lower than that of the whites... (O)n the one hand, the Negroes' plane of living is kept down by discrimination from the side of the whites while, on the other hand, the whites' reason for discrimination is partly dependent on the Negroes' plane of living. The Negroes' poverty, ignorance, superstition, slum dwellings, health deficiencies, dirty appearance, disorderly conduct, bad odor and criminality stimulate and feed the antipathy of the whites for them. 'Further, he noted that the Negroes' 'plane of living' was a 'composite entity.' It was affected by multiple variables – among them, 'employment,' 'wages,' 'housing,' 'nutrition,' 'health,' 'education,' and so on. A change in any one of these variables would have an effect on the others. Thus, for example, 'a rise in employment will tend to increase earnings, raise standards of living, and improve health, education, manners and law observance, and vice versa; a better education is assumed to raise the chances of a higher salaried job, and vice versa; and so all through our whole system of variables.' Given these interdependencies, he concluded that '*any change in any one of these factors, independent of the way it is brought about, will, by the aggregate weight of the cumulative effects running back and forth between them all, start the whole system moving in one direction or the other as the case may be*...'[14] Cumulative causation could, of course, work in either of two ways: as a 'vicious circle' or as a 'virtuous circle.'

In combination, this range of considerations provided the intellectual props to Myrdal's projection that the prospects for the advance on the part of the American Negro population were bullish. The centrality of the 'American creed' in the national consciousness – and the tensions between the ideal and the real – generated momentum for change. The key was the impact on the nation's conscience based on Myrdal's conviction that moral ideas had force. Once a change in the positive direction had been accomplished, cumulative causation would provide the dynamic leading to further improvement.

The encyclopedic dimensions of *An American Dilemma*

Myrdal's analysis of the propulsion inherent in the 'American creed' accounted for much of the book's force. But the two volumes in which the work was first published conveyed a lot more. A substantial body of the text chronicled details of white–black relations as they had evolved over the decades, as well as statistical data on factors affecting the Negroes' 'level of living.' Much of this documentation was drawn from the monographs commissioned in the first stage of the study.

An arresting segment of the text developed at some length an attribute of inter-racial perceptions not to be found in the commissioned research. Myrdal referred to this as the 'rank order of discriminations.' As far as Southern whites were concerned, the priorities for discrimination were ordered as follows:

1. the bar against intermarriage and sexual intercourse involving white women;
2. etiquettes and discriminations in personal relations, such as barriers against dancing, bathing, eating, and drinking together;
3. segregation in public facilities: for example, schools, churches, transport;
4. political disenfranchisement;
5. discrimination in law courts, say by the police;
6. discrimination in buying land, access to jobs, and credit.[15]

Myrdal found that the Negroes' rank order of discriminations was '*just about parallel, but inverse to that of the white man.*' Thus, their top priority was the elimination of discrimination in economic opportunity, followed by equality before the law. Voting rights came next and then improvement in the schools. Non-discrimination in sexual matters was '*of rather distant and doubtful interest.*'[16] There was an upbeat aspect to this finding. At least potentially, it suggested that there was a basis for negotiation when matters that whites cared least about were those that Negroes cared most about.

As Myrdal had pointed out in the preface to the work, his indebtedness to monograph contributors could be observed in the footnotes. Ralph Bunche was cited far more frequently than any other author. His fieldwork – in the South particularly where he had exposed himself to considerable personal hazards – was drawn on extensively. Especially valuable were his insights into the shady techniques for Negro disenfranchisement. Myrdal had the highest regard for Bunche as an empirical researcher and as a friend. The two men, however, did not see eye-to-eye on the direction for Negro political empowerment. Bunche held that the Negroes' natural allies were working class whites and that they should make common cause in mobilizing their economic class interests. Myrdal totally rejected the Marxist overtones of that line of argument. This was reminiscent of the way he had dismissed Marxism as a barren ideology when writing *The Political Element in the Development of Economic Theory*. The best hope for Negroes could more promisingly be realized through alliance with white liberals in the middle and upper classes who were conscience-stricken by shortfalls in the fulfillment of values articulated in the 'American creed.'

The closing chapter of *An American Dilemma* reflected a further consideration bearing on the timeliness of advancement in the status of the Negro population. Circumstances of World War II gave urgency to this matter. American leadership should now be a beacon to the entire world. Myrdal then wrote,

> If America in actual practice could show the world a progressive trend by which the Negro became finally integrated into modern democracy, all mankind would be given faith again – it would have reason to believe that peace, progress and order are feasible. And America would have spiritual power many times stronger than all her financial and military resources – the power of trust and support of all good people on earth. *America is free to choose whether the Negro shall remain her liability or become her opportunity.*[17]

Having delivered the bulk of the manuscript, Myrdal and Sterner returned to Sweden. There were still gaps to be filled and Arnold Rose was charged to close them. Myrdal left him with one categorical instruction. The last word in the book should be 'Enlightenment.' Having probed the depths of so much social misery, he regarded it as imperative to close on a positive note. And so it was. The final paragraph reads as follows:

> To find the practical formulas for this never-ending reconstruction of society is the supreme task of social science. The world catastrophe places tremendous difficulties in our way and may shake our confidence to the depths. Yet we have today in social science a greater trust in the improvement of man and society than we have ever had since the Enlightenment.[18]

The initial reception

An American Dilemma was published in January 1944. One might have expected this event to have been accompanied by a publicity campaign orchestrated by the Carnegie Corporation. This did not happen. Several factors may throw light on this apparent lapse. Frederick Keppel's departure from the Carnegie Presidency in 1942 – initially for government service in Washington – and his death in 1943 removed the project's most enthusiastic inside supporter. His successors in the leadership of the philanthropy were less than fully invested in the program. And they may have sensed some potential awkwardness had they chosen to promote a massive document of social commentary in wartime on a sensitive national issue.[19] They may also have chosen to assume a low profile because the final product was light years removed from what the Carnegie Corporation originally thought it was commissioning, that is, a modest report to aid in identifying priorities for grant-making in support of Negro advancement. Self-evidently, *An American Dilemma* did not satisfy that purpose.[20]

In early 1944, publication of *An American Dilemma* was hailed enthusiastically in the popular media. The *New York Herald Tribune* and *Time magazines*, for example, placed Myrdal in the company of Tocqueville and James Bryce – foreigners all – who had produced especially penetrating commentaries on American society.[21] This was select company indeed. Similar praise resonated in the endorsement of Reinhold Niebuhr, Dean of American Protestant theologians, who urged adoption of the book as a text for study groups sponsored by churches. It was also well received by leading Negro intellectuals of the time. E. Franklin Frazier and W. E. B. Du Bois, for example, applauded Myrdal's attack on segregation and discrimination.[22] Liberal white Southerners saw problems in the book, particularly in what they perceived to be the author's limited understanding of Southern history and culture, but they were generally muted in their criticism. Myrdal almost – but not quite – got a free pass from Southern segregationists. Mississippi's race-baiting Senator Theodore Bilbo attacked him for implying that society would be better off if it were composed of 'mixbreeds'; otherwise the hard-core racists were quiet. (Myrdal regarded this outcome as an indication that segregationists did not read hefty scholarly tomes.) Reviews in the academic journals, for the most part, were friendly. Few of the first team of the country's social scientists with expertise in racial matters, however, contributed to the public discussion. Most regarded themselves as disqualified as reviewers on the grounds that they had been on the Carnegie Corporation's payroll in the initial phases of the project.[23]

Perhaps the most biting negative criticism came from the pen of a sometime member of Myrdal's stable of researchers. Doxey Wilkerson, professor of sociology at Howard University, had contributed a fragment on 'The Negro in American Education' to the initial monographic phase. Wilkerson, however, suppressed mention of this association when writing a preface to a Marxist critique of *An American Dilemma*. He characterized the book as 'pretentious' and 'dangerous.' The study, he noted, was 'corporation financed.' (This was clearly a cheap shot. By choice of nomenclature, the Carnegie philanthropy was a 'Corporation,' but the implication that it was driven to maximize profits was manifestly incorrect.) He scolded reviewers who had described the work as 'monumental and definitive,' insisting that the Negro question was not – as Myrdal had maintained – a 'moral' issue. Instead Negro oppression was a by-product of 'the stark material, profit-seeking core' of the American economy.[24] This theme was sustained in the Marxist critique written by Herbert Aptheker who produced the tract that Wilkerson had introduced. Aptheker concluded that 'the Negro question was basically a material one, not a moral one. Oppression and the super-exploitation of the American Negro – and the prejudice based thereon – exist and are maintained because they were and are profitable and useful to America's propertied interests.'[25] Myrdal's rejection of Marxist determinism and his insistence that the moral ideas had both an authentic autonomy and the power to move events made him an obvious target for the ideological left.

An American Dilemma became the Bible of the liberal orthodoxy on racial matters in the two decades following the end of World War II. It provided part of the intellectual prop to the Supreme Court's decision in the Brown vs. the Topeka Board of Education case in 1954. This ruling held that racial segregation in tax-supported schools was unconstitutional. *An American Dilemma* was cited for supplying a rationale for the Court's unanimous decision. This was the first occasion in the twentieth century when a work of social science had figured in the Supreme Court's jurisprudence. This case was self-evidently one that grabbed headlines. But it should also be noted that a Myrdalian mentality could be detected in earlier rulings from the Federal bench. Extended quotations from *An American Dilemma* appeared in briefs filed in cases that struck down all-white primaries in the South and segregation of Negroes in dining cars on inter-state railroads.[26]

Actions of Federal courts attracted attention to the book in the Deep South. Senator James O. Eastland of Mississippi, for example, published a tirade denouncing a book by an author who 'had no knowledge of the Negro question in the United States' but who was driven by 'an alien ideology' in company with associates who were linked to Communist front activities. (As far as Doxey Wilkerson was concerned, there was substance to the latter charge.) The Supreme Court, Eastland concluded, had been 'brainwashed' and the South was not obligated to obey its decision. Eastland's polemic, however, did not play well outside the Deep South.[27]

In a preface written in 1962 in preparation for a twentieth anniversary edition, Myrdal struck a self-congratulatory note. He drew attention to his projection in 1944 of 'fundamental changes in American race relations, changes which will involve a development toward American ideals.' And he added,

> At that time I had little backing for this conclusion in the contemporary literature on the Negro problem in America, nor could I feel myself to have much support from the social scientists then working in the field of race relations, whose views in the main were more static, fatalistic, and more particularly, lacking in an appreciation of the importance for social change of the moral, ideological, and political forces in the nation. A student who has often been wrong in his forecasts will be excused for pointing to a case when he was right.'[28]

Harvard's Oscar Handlin welcomed this reissue in a review entitled 'A Book That Changed American Life,' observing that 'its analysis of the Negro problem in the United States has been a magnet to scholars and a catalyst to political groups.'[29]

In the early 1960s, a sense of satisfaction about this project seemed to be well grounded. Not only had *An American Dilemma* influenced the Supreme Court's decision on the evils of segregated schools, its arguments were also solidly in harmony with the thinking of key figures in the Civil Rights Movement. Its spirit seemed to have been incarnated, for example, in the activism of Martin Luther King, Jr, of Rosa Parks, and of the Freedom Riders of both races.

A sea change in the mid-1960s and 1970s

An American Dilemma was premised on the view that Negroes aspired to join the mainstream and would do so if the discriminatory barriers that excluded them were brought down. Beginning in the mid-1960s, the validity of that central premise was less than self-evident when a segment of the Negro population turned its back on the cultural mainstream. This challenge found its way into the headlines, for example, through the speeches of Black Muslim leaders and in the behavior of outstanding and highly visible Negro athletes: The world heavyweight champion changed his name from Cassius Clay to Mohammad Ali; the Hall-of-Fame basketball player Lew Alcindor became Kareem Abdul-Jabbar; Olympic track champions raised clenched fists when awarded medals on the victory platform.

In *An American Dilemma*, Myrdal had recognized instances of 'divergences' of Negro culture from the one predominant in the white community. But, he argued, that

> even the positive movement away from American culture has its source in that culture. Negro race pride and race prejudice serve to fortify the Negro against white superiority. *In practically all its divergence, American Negro culture is not something independent of general American culture. It is a distorted development, or a pathological condition, of the general American culture.*[30]

It should come as no surprise that some readers in the mid-1960s and beyond would find this language demeaning in its implication that Negro culture was lacking in intrinsic merit.

In 1944, Ralph Ellison (who was to produce a widely acclaimed novel, *Invisible Man*) wrote a review of *An American Dilemma* in which he observed,

> Myrdal sees Negro culture and personality simply as the product of a 'social pathology.' Thus, he assumes that 'it is to the advantage of American Negroes as individuals and as a group to become assimilated into American culture, to acquire the traits held in esteem by the dominant white Americans.' This, he admits, contains the value premise that 'here in America, American culture is "highest" in the pragmatic sense . . . ' Which aside from implying that Negro culture is not also American assumes that Negroes should desire nothing better than what whites consider highest. But in the 'pragmatic sense'

> lynching and Hollywood, faddism and radio advertising are products of the 'higher' culture, and the Negro might ask, 'why, if my culture is pathological, must I exchange it for these?'[31]

This assessment was written in 1944, but Ellison chose not to publish it until 20 years later. In 1966, Ellison again addressed this concern. He then argued,

> I defend the subculture, because I have to work out of it, because it is precious to me, because I believe it is a vital contributing part of the total culture. I do not think that I want to deny that. If I did, I would have to throw away my typewriter and become a sociologist... I wish that we would dispense with this idea that we are begging to get *in* somewhere. The mainstream is in oneself. The mainstream of American literature is in me, even though I am a Negro, because I possess more of Mark Twain than many white writers do.[32]

Ellison correctly identified a limitation in Myrdal's perspective. With respect to jazz, for example, Myrdal was tone-deaf.

Yet another consideration left a mark on revisionist readings of *An American Dilemma* in the 1970s and beyond. In particular, questions were raised about whether or not Myrdal had exaggerated the impact of the 'American creed' on the nation's conscience. To be sure, the shaping of the book was influenced by the historical circumstances surrounding its creation. The conception of an 'American creed' during and immediately after World War II had considerable force. The ideals it represented stood in sharp contrast to the doctrines espoused as Nazism and fascism. Myrdal's depiction of the 'American creed's' vitality captured a significant feature of the national mood at that time. But whether this mood could flourish in all seasons was debatable. The subsequent flow of events – notably, the political polarization generated by wars in Vietnam and latterly in Iraq, the Watergate scandals – has considerably diminished the average citizen's faith in the redemptive power of the civic religion articulated by the Founding Fathers.

For his part, Myrdal maintained his faith in the potency of the 'American creed.' He continued to regard the country as his second home. He would be outspoken in his criticisms of the follies of its government. This was the case when he decried US policies toward East–West trade in the 1950s and, still more forcefully, when he attacked its prosecution of the Vietnam War. At the time when the Watergate scandal was exposed – and when the national morale was certainly at a low ebb – he was interviewed in Stockholm by a journalist writing for *Today's Health* (an organ of the American Medical Association). The reaction to Watergate 'underline[d] [his] conception of what American democracy is all about. . . . In America, truth will out. America is an open society. When the system discovered Watergate, it did something about it – a lot, in fact.' When asked to comment further on this phenomenon, he observed, 'It's a conversion, really, and conversions are very much a part of American history. You can go very, very wrong for a while, but then you can change overnight. . . . I don't know of any country that is more prepared to switch policies than America.' He concluded by saying that 'American society is still a wide-open society, thank God, and it will be even more so after this. I still believe that this deep sense of moral behavior is the essence of America – that it is the glory of the nation, its youthful strength, and, in the end, perhaps the salvation of mankind.'[33]

An American Dilemma revisited?

In November 1971, Myrdal announced his intention to return to the study of the Negro problem in the United States. The occasion was a visit to Harvard University to deliver an invited lecture. He used this as an opportunity to meet staff members of the University's recently constructed program in Afro-American studies. 'I consider this a very important assignment,' he was reported as saying. He hoped to complete it in a couple of years 'if God gives me the time to do it.'[34]

Preliminary arrangements were made to engage Kenneth Clark, the Negro social psychologist who had participated in the original project, as a collaborator. This exercise did not mature: The two men had a falling-out. For a time, Myrdal proceeded with this revisitation on his own. He remained uncompromising in his conviction that assimilation of blacks into the American mainstream was the correct course. And he vigorously opposed programs that afforded preferential treatment of Negroes. He maintained that 'it would be most unfortunate to try to get a kind of Marshall Plan specifically for the Negro.' What was needed, he maintained, was action 'to lift *all* the poor people at the bottom . . . out of poverty and everything that poverty implies.'[35] In 1977, he reported as follows on the status of the project:

> Now after more than 30 years I have returned to the problems of race relations in America with *An American Dilemma Revisited: The Racial Crisis in the United States in Perspective.* I have taken the findings in the old book as a firm baseline for the study of the dynamics in more recent decades. I decided to use again the ideals of the American creed as the instrumental value premises. In what meanwhile has happened to race relations in America, I find no reason to surrender my contention that a gradually ever-fuller realization of the ideals contained in that national ethos is more than a selected viewpoint when observing and analyzing the facts; it is and will remain the trend of historical change in this country – in a sense the destiny of America, if America is not going to give up its essential national personality.[36]

Suffering from Parkinson's disease and deteriorating eyesight, seeing this project through to completion proved to be beyond his declining powers. There was a sense of personal disappointment about this outcome, though there need not have been. He had already contributed more than enough to this line of inquiry for one lifetime. *An American Dilemma* had, after all, been a catalytic agent in opening doors for black advancement. In the process, American society had been transformed with blacks in positions of authority in every branch of social and professional life. This improvement has been uneven – a sizeable underclass (heavily black, but not exclusively so) did not share in it. Nonetheless, in the social commentaries of prominent blacks – such as the actor-entertainer Bill Cosby, or Bob Herbert, the *New York Times* columnist – which are scathing in their denunciations of black parents who tolerate hip-hop or ghetto speech by their offspring (as opposed to nurturing them into the mainstream), one can detect overtones of the voice of Gunnar Myrdal.

Notes

1. By way of illustration, *Saturday Review* in 1964 invited a panel of prominent intellectuals to respond to the following question: 'What books published during the last four decades most significantly altered the direction of our society?' *An American Dilemma* placed second only to John Maynard Keynes's *General Theory of Employment, Interest, and Money*. See R. Girson, 'Mutations in the Body Politic,' *Saturday Review* (29 August 1964), 74–82.
2. F. P. Keppel to G. Myrdal, 12 August 1937, as quoted in *An American Dilemma*, p. ix.
3. G. Myrdal to F. P. Keppel, 28 January 1939, as quoted in ibid.
4. Ralph Bunche was the first Negro to be awarded the Nobel Peace Prize, which was accorded to him in 1950 for his diplomatic work in peacemaking in the Middle East as an official of the United Nations.
5. Among them, M. J. Herskovits, *The Myth of the Negro Past* (1941); C. S. Johnson, *Patterns of Negro Segregation* (1943); R. Sterner, *The Negro's Share* (1943). R. Bunche's substantial monographs were published posthumously in 1973 under the title *The Political Status of the Negro in the Age of FDR* by the University of Chicago Press.
6. As quoted by B. Urquhart, *Ralph Bunche: An American Life* (New York and London: W. W. Norton and Co., 1993), p. 81.
7. G. and A. Myrdal, *Kontakt med Amerika*, p. 33 (excerpts translated by Anna Ankar Barron).
8. Ibid., p. 52.
9. Ibid., p. 54, as quoted by W. A. Jackson, *Gunnar Myrdal and America's Conscience: Social Engineering and Racial Liberalism, 1938–1987* (Chapel Hill: University of North Carolina Press, 1990), p. 151.
10. Jackson, op. cit., p. 148.
11. G. Myrdal, 'Introduction,' p. xlvii. Italics in the original.
12. G. Myrdal, 'Author's Preface,' p. xix. Italics in the original.
13. Appendix 2, 'Note on Facts and Valuations,' p. 1045. Italics in the original.
14. 'A Methodological Note on the Principle of Cumulation,' Appendix 3, pp. 1066–67.
15. *An American Dilemma*, pp. 60–61.
16. Ibid., p. 61. Italics in the original.
17. Ibid., pp. 1021–22. Italics in the original.
18. Ibid., p. 1024.
19. In 1975, the then Secretary of the Carnegie Corporation observed that 'the Corporation's failure to follow up on the Myrdal study is perhaps the greatest missed opportunity in its history, one that can be regretted now in hindsight' (as quoted by Ellen Condliffe Lagemann, *The Politics of Knowledge: The Carnegie Corporation, Philanthropy, and Public Policy* (Middletown, Connecticut: Wesleyan University Press, 1989), p. 146.
20. A number of these points have been noted by S. R. Graubard, 'Preface to *An American Dilemma Revisited*,' *Daedalus* (Winter 1995).

21. A. de Tocqueville (1805–1859) was a French aristocrat with liberal views. His *Democracy in America* – based on a tour of the United States in 1830 – was published in two volumes. The first appeared in 1835, the second in 1840. James Bryce (1838–1922), sometime professor of law in the University of Oxford and Liberal member of the British Parliament, wrote *The American Commonwealth*, initially published in 1888, which subsequently went through multiple editions. He served as British Ambassador to the United States from 1907 to 1913 and was the only foreigner to be elected to the Presidency of the American Political Science Association.
22. As the elder statesman among Negro intellectuals, Du Bois's comments deserve special note. He wrote as follows: 'Never before in American history has a scholar so completely covered this field. Myrdal does not gag at facts.... He does not appease the South.... He does not attempt to be 'scientific' in the sense of depending solely upon such facts as lend themselves to accurate mathematical measurement. In other words, the sociology of Myrdal emancipates itself from physical and biological and psychological analogies, and openly and frankly takes into account emotions, thoughts, opinions and ideals.' W. E. B. Du Bois, *'The American Dilemma,' Phylon: The Atlanta University Review of Race and Culture*, 5 (Second Quarter 1944), 121–22.
23. For comprehensive surveys of the book's reception, see W. A. Jackson, op. cit., pp. 241–71, and D. W. Southern, *Gunnar Myrdal and Black-White Relations: The Use and Abuse of 'An American Dilemma'* (Baton Rouge and London: Louisiana State University Press, 1987), especially Chapter 4.
24. On these points, see Southern, op. cit., especially Chapter 6.
25. D. A. Wilkerson, 'Introduction' to H. Aptheker, *The Negro People in America: A Critique of Gunnar Myrdal's An American Dilemma* (New York: International Publishers, 1946), pp. 7–8.
26. H. Aptheker, op. cit., p. 66.
27. O. Handlin, 'A Book That Changed American Life,' *New York Times Book Review* (21 April 1963) 1, 24–5.
28. Senator J. O. Eastland, 'An Alien Ideology Is Not the Law of Our Republic,' The American Mercury (March 1958) 28–9.
29. G. Myrdal, 'Author's Preface to the Twentieth Anniversary Edition,' p. xxiii.
30. Ibid., p. 928. Italics in the original.
31. R. Ellison, *Shadow and Act* (New York: Random House, 1964), p. 316.
32. R. Ellison, as quoted by S. R. Graubard, 'Preface,' *An American Dilemma Revisited, Daedalus* (Winter 1995), xxviii.
33. G. Myrdal, 'Therapy to Heal America's Wounded Psyche,' *Today's Health*, 51 (August 1973) 16–19, 63–64.
34. *New York Times* (6 November 1971) 33.
35. G. Myrdal in 'Liberalism and the Negro: a Round-Table Discussion,' *Commentary* (March 1964) 30.
36. G. Myrdal, *The Christian Century*, 14 December 1977 (as reproduced in *Current*, 202 [April 1978] 51).

7
Minister of Commerce and Economic Policy-Making for Post-War Sweden, 1944–1947

Leaving Arnold Rose behind to plug the last holes in the manuscript of *An American Dilemma*, Myrdal returned to Sweden in the autumn of 1942. He quickly re-engaged with Swedish politics. In 1943, he was re-elected to the seat for Dalarna in the Swedish Senate that he had vacated some 5 years earlier. He resumed this position in January 1944. He was also appointed to chair a Commission on Post-war Economic Planning. This body recommended that full employment should be the government's paramount goal and urged that public spending on housing should be the primary instrument for balancing the economy to achieve this objective.[1]

For a period of approximately 4 months (late August to mid-November) in 1943, he found himself back in the United States. His mission this time was to assess the post-war prospects of the American economy at the behest of the Swedish Foreign Office. He conducted extensive interviews with leading public officials, with influential figures in the business community, with trade unionists, as well as with members of the first team in academic economics and other social sciences. He also enjoyed the unusual experience of being presented on the floor of the US Senate by Vice-President Henry A. Wallace.

Evaluating post-war prospects for the American economy

Myrdal reported his findings from this expedition to a meeting of the National Economic Society of Sweden in March 1944. (An English-language version of this talk appeared in the *Atlantic Monthly* in November 1944 under the title 'Is American Business Deluding

Itself?') The substance of his statement was sobering. He described it as a 'cold-blooded analysis.'[2] The economic policies of the New Deal in the 1930s had been failures when judged against the objectives of restoring full production and employment. The war had been responsible for the increased aggregate demand necessary to bring the economy to full capacity operations. Admittedly, the productive achievements spawned by the war had been outstanding. With the war's end not too distantly in prospect, it was vital to come to grips with the issue of whether or not a similar achievement could be sustained in peacetime. For his part, Myrdal expressed amazement about the degree of optimism he found in American opinion about the post-war maintenance of prosperity. It reminded him of the naive faith in permanent prosperity that he had encountered when first visiting the United States in 1929.

If one looked at the practical realities, the dimensions of the challenge that the country would face appeared to be staggering. Government expenditures – almost exclusively in support of the war effort – accounted for roughly half of the nation's GNP. With the end of hostilities, these outlays would be sharply curtailed. A massive exercise in converting the economy's structure from production for war to production for peace would necessarily follow. This would involve major cutbacks in jobs in the war-related sectors. Pressure on the labor market would be further intensified with demobilization of most of the eleven-and-a-half million service men and women. He drew on the analytic framework developed by Harvard's Alvin H. Hansen – who by this time was universally recognized as America's leading Keynesian – to explore the implications of reconversion for the employment picture and concluded that they were deficient by virtue of being too static. '*It presupposes full employment,*' he wrote, 'and then studies the direction of demand for manpower required for realizing this presupposition.'[3] This line of analysis, he maintained, was flawed because 'it is not at all concerned with how the whole procedure is to be brought about – *by developments over a period of time*'. Further, if one assumed that '*there will not be full employment,* then the release of manpower in industry will be greater in all industries and the possibility of providing the unemployed with new jobs will be less everywhere.'[4]

Myrdal recognized that the American situation contained some features favorable for the prospects of prosperity, though he believed that their force would be insufficient to ward off a substantial downturn in economic activity for long. A return to peacetime conditions would reveal heavy pent-up demand for durable household appliances and for automobiles. The war had halted production of these items. Meanwhile, the public at large was in a strong liquidity position, owing to savings that had been allocated to the purchase of war bonds that could instantly be converted to cash. In addition, sustained demand for subsidized American exports – particularly for agricultural commodities – to war-devastated parts of the world could be expected for a time with their distribution managed by the United Nations Relief and Rehabilitation Agency.

These positive influences on aggregate demand were fairly short-term, however, and would soon be expected to wear off. Meanwhile they would at least partially be neutralized by unfavorable aspects in the situation. Myrdal expected substantial labor-management turmoil to be a part of the post-war scenario. Wages in the war industries, he observed, had been unusually high, but these sectors were to be phased out. Employers in the more conventional industries – many of whom had experienced a profit squeeze during the regime of war-time price controls – would be eager to put downward pressure on average wage scales. The picture Myrdal sketched was not pretty. He described the likely scene as follows:

> If. . . we take into account the vast unrest accompanying the conversion procedure, mass unemployment in the war-industry areas, and the probably very confused internal political situation, the result may be a radicalization of labor opinion and actual conflicts on the labor front.

'And he also struck a note that was at odds with the guiding perspective of *An American Dilemma*: 'Unfortunately, we must even contemplate that the race question may emerge in its most terrifying form. An epidemic of violence, expressed in bloody fights on the part of labor, will, without regard to the more direct consequences, have a depressing influence on the development of the business cycle.'[5]

Myrdal anticipated that there would be yet another cloud on the American economic horizon – one that was a by-product of the government's program of building large-scale facilities to produce war-related goods, followed by assignment of larger firms to operate them. He presumed that 'this socialized section' of American industry would be sold off to the private sector and that the massive corporations would be the big winners. This inclined him to predict that 'a hard struggle with many complications is to be expected on the monopoly front.'[6]

The considerations above led him to conclude the following:

> It is to be expected that America after the war in Europe will experience a high degree of economic unrest. There will be shortages in certain fields and unemployment in others.... There will certainly be mass unemployment in large areas. Great difficulties are likely to arise on the labor market. Yet it is possible that a 'sellers' market' will be established so generally as to avoid an immediate post-war slump. But, probably within the period of, let us say, from half a year to three years, this development would change over into slump. This slump may turn out to be a culmination of the deflationary crisis of the early twenties and the gigantic crisis between 1929 and 1932.[7]

There was nothing preordained about the inevitability of this outcome. Myrdal insisted that he did 'not deny the theoretical possibility of establishing an economic plan capable of fulfilling the optimistic hopes about stabilized full employment. (B)ut... political development in America is likely to be away from planning, rather than toward it.'[8]

Toward educating Swedish opinion

In 1944, Myrdal addressed a book-length study – entitled *Varning för fredsoptimism* (Warning for Peace Optimism) – to his fellow Swedes. He began by asserting that he was offering a 'hard-boiled analysis.' This was not intended as a statement of disrespect for America, a country which he held in high esteem, despite his skepticism about its capacity to maintain a high level of economic activity in the post-war world. 'I have considered it my duty,' he wrote, 'to warn my compatriots of two great illusions: that the Americans will succeed in stabilizing their post-war economy; and that the Americans and the British will succeed, by themselves and with others, in building a satisfactory international economic order.' He summed up his appraisal of the prospects ahead as follows:

> In my view, everything seems to indicate that America after the war will be entering a very unstable economic development which soon enough will fall into a depression with mass unemployment. Furthermore, unfortunately, the chances are great that all the beautiful plans for the liberalization and stabilization of the world's economy will be empty promises and that essentially the international problems will remain when peace "breaks out." This would mean a worse world economic order than the one that existed before the war.[9]

The substantive argument of *Warning for Peace Optimism* was an extended elaboration of the case he had set out in the *Atlantic Monthly* article entitled 'Is American Business Deluding Itself?'. But there was a coda that spoke specifically to Swedish conditions. 'Sweden's interest in the dangerous post-war world,' he argued, 'will simply be survival. Just as now during the war, our most urgent task will be to secure our existence as a free nation.' He anticipated that the challenges would be formidable. The derangement of the world economy meant that the country would need to 'drive a hard bargain' in its conduct of international trade policy. The country would be lucky if its exports were not discriminated against. Inconvertible currencies and trade barriers would put brakes on recovery and expansion throughout Europe. He concluded with the observation that

> nobody knows how lengthy this post-war crisis will be, nor what will come after it. It is not at all unlikely that after two years of scarcity of imported goods but good demand for our exports, there will come another period when imported goods will accumulate as freely as during the Thirties, while a general world depression simultaneously presses our export opportunities down.[10]

Articulating Sweden's foreign economic policy as a cabinet member

In mid-1945, Parliamentary elections produced a Swedish government fully under the control of the Social Democratic Party.

Throughout most of the war years, a national-unity government had ruled the country, though with the Social Democrats as senior partners. Myrdal was appointed to the cabinet as Minister of Commerce in the first post-war regime. His predecessor in that office had been Bertil Ohlin, a Conservative and fellow member of the Stockholm School.

In December 1946, Myrdal delivered a major address to the National Economic Society in Stockholm in which he reviewed main features of Sweden's foreign economic policy during his watch. The arrival of V-E Day, he noted, did not signal any near-term prospect that ante-bellum trade patterns and practices could be resumed. Germany – a principal source of Sweden's imports and a major outlet for its exports before the war – was an economic basket case. Meanwhile turmoil throughout Europe – in which individual countries sought to repair wartime destruction behind the shelters of trade barriers and inconvertible currencies – did not augur well for an early return to 'normality.' For its part, Sweden had attempted to ease burdens, especially for its Nordic neighbors, through reconstruction assistance. It recognized the necessity – however unfortunate that might be – of direct controls over exports and imports in the larger European economic environment. For this reason, it had actively negotiated a series of bilateral trade agreements with trading partners. This was a step down from the ideal: Sweden's principled and traditional commitment to openness in international trade and payments remained its ultimate policy objective. But compromise on this point was an inescapable concession to the reality.

He spoke in detail to a particular trade agreement: the one he had negotiated for Sweden with the Soviet Union. The Swedish government included substantial credits to the Soviets in this package. The announcement of this decision did nothing for the government's popularity in the electorate. Much of the business community was hostile and it became a tinderbox issue in the popular press. Much of the citizenry – erroneously, in Myrdal's opinion – associated domestic shortages with earmarkings of goods for export to the Soviet Union. He referred to the 'distorted discussion' of the Russian Trade Agreement that had 'served to fortify . . . false ideas.' And he added,

> The public was in fact given the impression that the scarcity of everything in this country – for instance, of nails, paper or bath tubs – and all restrictions – e.g., a town's not being allowed to build

> a ski-run or to organize an exhibition or to erect as many houses as were actually needed – *were due to* 'The Russian Agreement'. In some mysterious fashion this was supposed to be the effect of the Agreement six months before it was concluded and long before any concrete supply contracts could possibly have been signed.[11]

The political rows touched off by the Russian Trade Agreement – which the Swedish Parliament had proceeded to ratify – proved to be Myrdal's undoing as a Cabinet Minister. Under the terms of the Agreement, Sweden provided substantial credits over a 5-year period to enable the Soviets to purchase precision equipment and machinery. These loans were to be repaid after 15 years.[12] A leading Stockholm editorialist and sometime Myrdal friend assailed the Agreement as running counter to Sweden's interest. Members of the family were subjected to personal attacks. Daughter Sissela recounts how she and her siblings – and not just their parents – were vilified.[13]

Myrdal was no stranger to controversy. At times he had actively courted it. He had done so when attacking the elders in Stockholm's economics establishment in *The Political Element in the Development of Economic Theory* and in his writings on the population crisis. But there were dimensions to this one that he had not met before. He resigned as Sweden's Minister of Commerce in March 1947.

The rationale

Myrdal's support for the Swedish–Soviet Trade Agreement was buttressed by a well-considered appraisal of the likely condition of the international economic environment, post-World War II. He had set it out in his writings in 1944. The prospect ahead, he then maintained, would be dominated by a reversion of the American economy toward its pre-war status with mass unemployment and underutilization of productive capacity. Sound economic policy for Sweden called for buffers against the ramifications of this phenomenon. Against this backdrop, sealing in a captive market for Sweden's exports – which was the main point of the Trade Agreement – made eminent sense. Bertil Ohlin, his predecessor at the Ministry of Commerce, concurred, as did Ernst Wigforss, the long-standing Minister of Finance in Social Democratic governments.

In Britain, there was a counterpart to this scenario. During World War II, the British government had accumulated a mass of liabilities that arose from local expenditures in parts of the world which had served as staging areas for military operations. These liabilities – known as the 'sterling balances' – were to be retired after the war on a timetable to be established by the British Treasury. (Egypt and India were the major holders of such balances.) One segment of British opinion believed that a successful appeal could have been launched in the flush of victory to write off these liabilities as a contribution to the common cause. The Labour government, led by Clement Atlee, that came to power in July 1945 chose not to push such an initiative. Its reasons for doing so had much in common with Swedish thinking that supported the Trade Agreement with the Soviet Union. Like Myrdal and his sympathetic colleagues, senior British economists engaged in shaping foreign economic policy for a Labour government were skeptical about the capacity of the United States to maintain full employment for long after the cessation of hostilities. It was therefore prudent to keep the sterling balances in place as a buffer against the impact of a downturn in the United States on the country's export markets. Winston Churchill, leader of the Conservative opposition in the late 1940s, would rail against this decision by asking how much longer would Britain need to pay Egypt for the privilege of defending her in World War II – but to no avail.

A touch of irony

Economists who had the ear of social democratic governments in both Sweden and Britain were at one in their suspicions about the prospects for stability and sustained prosperity in the unplanned economy that would be post-World War II America. Their views about the proper conduct of international economic policy were embedded within this intellectual framework.

In the Soviet Union a quite different voice was heard. It came from Eugen Varga, a Hungarian by birth, who had compiled a distinguished record of contributions to Soviet economics. He produced an essay entitled *Changes in the Economy of Capitalism Resulting from World War II,* in which he argued that Marxist theoreticians would be well advised to revise their expectations about the downfall of capitalism on the grounds that the World War II had changed the character of capitalist systems. Successful conduct of the war effort, he maintained, had demanded extensive state intervention in economic life. Though the role of the state could be expected to diminish in peacetime, lessons learned from wartime economic planning would not be completely forgotten. In his view, an active role for governments as regulators and stabilizers had come to stay and the days of swashbuckling capitalist 'anarchy' had passed. For these reasons, Western capitalism could be expected to be more stable after the war than it had been before. These views conflicted sharply with official Soviet doctrine. Varga was sharply censured and relieved of his official positions.

It is passing strange that Varga's prognostications about the post-war course of Western – and particularly American – capitalism came closer to capturing the reality than did those of British and Swedish economists advising social democratic governments. In defense of the latter, however, it must be emphasized that America's foreign economic policy – post-war – took turns that could not reasonably have been anticipated in 1945–1946. At the end of the war, for example, no credible forecaster would have bet on the U-turn in a long-standing tradition in America's foreign policy represented by the Marshall Plan. (In Winston Churchill's judgment, this was 'the most unsordid act in history'.) Nor can the pessimists about the future of the American economy reasonably be faulted for failing to foresee other significant props to aggregate demand – the post-war baby boom and the spur to government spending occasioned by the cold war.

Roughly a decade after he had gone on record with his flawed forecast of the post-war behavior of the American economy, Myrdal published a post-mortem on this episode. In 1955, he wrote,

> Economists generally, including the present author, feared towards the end of the war that in the normal course of business development the United States was likely to experience a serious business depression after the very accentuated war boom. We were mistaken. The United States has instead – with some minor intermittent recessions – enjoyed a remarkably steady progress and showed a resilience to change which in the beginning of the period cannot be explainsed in terms of the effects of high expenditures for armaments. This, and certain experiences in Western Europe in

> recent years that do not fit any better our concepts of business fluctuations, have convinced me that we need a radical overhaul of the entire theoretical framework within which we analyze short-term economic movements, including the whole complicated system of analysis which for the sake of brevity I might be permitted to call 'post-Keynesian.' I believe a critical analysis could very usefully start by asking why and how we went wrong.

Myrdal also provided a partial answer to his own question and it had something in common with Eugen Varga's reasoning:

> Among changes brought about by – or during – the Second World War are the entirely changed role of governments in economic life, the changed economic philosophies steering the policies of governments and various public organs in their reactions to business fluctuations, possibly also a changed pattern of reactions on the part of business – though we do not know as yet much about this factor – and, in particular, a different system of functional relations between actual changes and expectations.

Notes

1. L. Magnusson, *An Economic History of Sweden* (London: Routledge, 2000), pp. 248–49.
2. G. Myrdal, 'Is American Business Deluding Itself?', *Atlantic Monthly*, 174 (November 1944) 51.
3. Ibid., 53.
4. Ibid.
5. Ibid., 57.
6. Ibid., 58.
7. Ibid.
8. Ibid.
9. G. Myrdal, *Varning för fredsoptimism* (Stockholm: Albert Bonniers förlag, 1944), p. 51. This translation from the Swedish and others from this document are by Anna Ankar Barron.
10. Ibid., pp. 345–48.
11. G. Myrdal, 'The Reconstruction of World Trade and Swedish Trade Policy,' English translation of a paper read to the Swedish National Economic Society, Stockholm, December 1946, Supplement B to the Svenska Handelsbanken Index, 1946. The Swedish version of that text contains a sentence following the paragraph quoted above that is omitted from the official English translation. A translation of the omitted material

by Anna Ankar Barron reads as follows: 'The news that exports, according to the new agreement, will be very insignificant during the most immediate scarcity period, was drowned in these suspicions vis-a-vis exports resulting from ignorance and considerable demagoguery'. ('Svenska handelspolitiken efter kriget,' *Fackföreningsrörelsen)* (July–December 1946, band 2.)

12. W. A. Jackson, *Gunnar Myrdal and America's Conscience* (Chapel Hill: University of North Carolina Press, 1991), p. 321.
13. S. Bok, *Alva Myrdal: A Daughter's Memoir* (Reading, MA: Addison-Wesley Publishing Co.), pp. 190–93.

8

International Civil Servant and Studies of the International Economy, 1947–1957

By the spring of 1947, it appeared that the brouhaha over Sweden's trade agreement with the Soviet Union had seriously compromised Myrdal's prospects for advancement in Swedish politics. It was fortuitous that an opportunity was then presented to him by Trygve Lie, Secretary-General of the United Nations, to head a new organization commissioned by the UN's Economic and Social Council. The entity in question was to be designated as the 'Economic Commission for Europe' (subsequently referred to as 'ECE'). This was the first regional organization to be created under the UN's auspices and it was followed by similar commissions for Asia and the Far East and for Latin America.

Myrdal was fully conscious of the magnitude of the challenges that a nascent ECE would confront. His appointment as its Executive Secretary, with headquarters in Geneva, at least had a non-trivial recommendation: It gave him a chance to put the bitterness associated with recent events in Sweden behind him. In his latter-day reflections about the international atmosphere in the spring of 1947, he observed,

> Back in 1947 when I accepted my post with the ECE, I certainly felt that an experiment in independent, disinterested research by an inter-governmental organization was worth making; but I did not regard it as certain or, perhaps, even very likely, that it would be possible in the political climate as it was after the Second World War to maintain freedom of research for a secretariat placed at the service, and under the direction, of so many

sovereign governments, all of which, at every juncture, must feel an intense opportunistic advantage in having their own, mutually conflicting, views of economic reality supported or at least not countered. And as I was not prepared to give up the attitude toward research that I have just stated, I did not expect – for this reason among others – to stay so long with the ECE.'[1]

The purpose and functions of the ECE

As specified by the UN's Economic and Social Council, the ECE was mandated to 'initiate and participate in measures for facilitating concerted action for the economic reconstruction of Europe, for raising the level of European economic activity, and for maintaining and strengthening the economic relations of the European countries both among themselves and with other countries of the world....' Further, the Commission was instructed to 'make or sponsor such investigations and studies of economic and technological problems and of developments within member countries of the Commission and within Europe generally as the Commission deems appropriate' as well as to 'undertake or sponsor the collection, evaluation and dissemination of such economic, technological and statistical information as the Commission deems appropriate.'[2]

The creation of the ECE at this particular moment in history was influenced by a number of factors: among them, the imminent demise of the United Nations Relief and Rehabilitation Agency (UNRRA) and a recognized need for an institution to succeed temporary European emergency economic organizations such as the European Coal Organization (ECO) and the European Central Inland Transport Organization (ECITO). Membership in the Commission was intended to be Europe-wide (with the exception of Spain, which was excluded). The United States was also a member on the strength of its status as an occupation authority in Germany.

The first meeting of the ECE was convened in May 1947 in a session devoted to a discussion of procedural issues. These matters were not successfully resolved on this occasion: business was scheduled to be resumed at a second session in July 1947. The climate for Europe-wide treatment of economic issues underwent a sea change between the dates of the ECE's first and second sessions. In June 1947, the American Secretary of State, George C. Marshall, announced an unprecedented initiative in which he called upon European nations to prepare a joint statement of their requirements for economic reconstruction, with the expectation that the United States would undertake to cover needs that could not be met through their pooled resources. The American offer was open-ended: the invitation drew no distinction between the countries of Western Europe, on the one hand, and the Soviet Union and its East European neighbors, on the other.

For a few brief moments, it appeared that the ECE might be called upon to perform a function that had not been anticipated when its terms of reference were drafted, namely to serve as an all-European authority to inventory Europe's needs and resources in response to Marshall's request. This aspiration was short-lived – it was a casualty of East–West tensions. The Soviet delegation walked out of a conference in Paris that was convened for the purpose of producing a collective reply to the American proposal, and representatives of East European governments went with them. The shaping of the Marshall Plan thus became a West European effort. Myrdal worked vigorously – but against the odds – to sustain the ECE as a vehicle that would transcend the East–West split in Europe. Toward that end, he insisted that his deputy as Executive Secretary should be a Russian national and that he would be a person of Myrdal's choice, not an appointee nominated by the Soviet government.[3] The man selected for this post was Nikolai Perovitch Koktomov, most recently counselor of the Soviet Embassy in London. When announcing the appointment, Myrdal observed that Koktomov 'has had wide experience in the diplomatic and executive fields both in his country and abroad' and that he brought to the ECE Secretariat 'a singularly valuable knowledge of economics and industry.'[4]

ECE activities in the early going

Even before its organizational structure had been fully formed, the ECE moved quickly to absorb the functions formerly assigned to the ECO, the ECITO, and the Emergency Economic Committee for Europe (EECE). As Executive Secretary, Myrdal pointed out that the ECE had 'inherited not only the problems left behind by the three emergency organizations...: it has inherited also the experience these organizations had gained in the field of post-war economic activity.'[5]

Committees staffed by officials with technical expertise were created to deal with problems associated with the availability of basic commodities, of which the most prominent was coal (which the ECE had the authority to allocate). Myrdal insisted on the importance of collaborative collegiality between members of the technical committees. On this matter, he remarked,

> It is quite naturally in everyone's interest that the experts in the various fields should not think, or plan, or act, in isolation. It is no good making provisions for the supply of coal, without taking into account the availability of transport. It is equally useless to make plans for the distribution of electric power without allowing for the supply of other fuels.

It was imperative for the individual experts to work together 'so that they can compare their problems and solve them in a spirit of general "give and take." '[6] By early 1948, the Executive Secretary was generally satisfied with the work of the expert committees whose members had been able to 'de-politicize' economic problems. 'In all our principal technical committees,' he reported, 'we have had no trouble over constitutional or procedural questions which are brought up when people don't want work to be done.'[7] Part of the reason why the technical committees had developed such a workmanlike atmosphere stemmed from the fact that the USSR and the Eastern Europeans had chosen not to participate. The political climate in the ECE's plenary sessions stood in marked contrast. Delegates from the Eastern bloc attended those meetings and, with their presence, the discussion tended to be dominated by inflammatory speeches denouncing the Marshall Plan and American economic imperialism.

When putting the ECE's organizational structure in place, Myrdal paid special attention to a Research and Planning Division which he characterized as the 'Keeper of the Commission's conscience.' Its activities would not be concerned with 'the work of international administration.' Instead, 'its function [would] be to provide the Commission and its committees with the necessary factual information on the economic situation in Europe, and to assist them in their study of specific problems.' He added that its work would fall into two parts:

> There will be a Survey Section which will shed light on the progress of reconstruction in European countries and on the main obstacles that limit the rate of economic improvement: manpower, raw materials, fuel and power, industrial capacity, and so forth. When the work of the Section is sufficiently advanced, it will issue a selective survey of Europe's economic position – selective in the sense that it will not attempt to cover the whole vast field, but will instead act as an alarm clock drawing the attention of European countries to impending difficulties and troubles.[8]

The 'Alarm Clock' in action

Throughout his decade as the ECE's Executive Secretary, Myrdal was blessed by the services of numerous cohorts of outstanding academic economists who staffed the Research and Planning Division. It rapidly acquired an enviable reputation as an intellectually stimulating 'think-tank' and that made it a magnet for talent. The appointment of Britain's Nicholas Kaldor, then at the London School of Economics (LSE), as the first Director of the Research and Planning Division was a stroke of good fortune. (The circumstances under which Kaldor took the job, however, were less than ideal. He had earlier been courted by the International Monetary Fund, and LSE had granted him 2 years' leave should he choose to accept. But, when he elected to join Myrdal in Geneva, LSE pressured him to resign.) The roster of other recruits to the Research and Planning Division was also impressive. It included Robert Neild, Ester and Mogens Boserup, Helen Makower, Albert Kervyn, Hans Staehle, Hal Lary, Tibor Barna, and P. J. Verdoorn.[9]

The Research and Planning Division's first major product – *A Survey of the Economic Situation and Prospects of Europe* – published in Geneva in 1948 attracted a wide readership. While it provided an overview of the general European situation, it also did much more. As Myrdal described it,

> The authors were among the first to draw attention to the special character of the serious post-war problems of 'suppressed

> inflation' in a number of countries, and they also devoted considerable attention to trade and balance of payments problems and to the possible conditions for an expansion of intra-European trade on a multilateral basis.[10]

Among the eager consumers of this product were American officials charged with the administration of the Marshall Plan.

Myrdal was ambitious to promote and sustain the prestige of the Research and Planning Division within the international community of economists. He was inclined to view its work environment as analogous to that of the academy. But he also recognized that the Division could not totally replicate 'pure' academic freedom. Its economists were, of course, obliged to be guided by the highest standards of disinterested and scientific professionalism. It would be wrong, however, to attempt to reproduce the academy in all its features. Research in the ECE, he argued,

> must always be 'practical' and directly 'useful'....(A) research institution of this type must necessarily try to concentrate on those issues where it can hope to make a positive contribution. It must refrain from deliberately picking out those where political relationships, either national or international, are so embroiled as to give little chance for improvement of policy through scientific inquiry.[11]

But Myrdal also believed that the ECE could play a useful leadership role in combating a tendency toward parochialism among European economists. Toward that end, he proposed to the Rockefeller Foundation that it finance periodic conferences which would bring 'together in their private capacities leading economists from various countries to discuss, in both their theoretical and practical aspects, major problems of the European economy.'[12] He set out the following rationale:

> The need for periodic meetings of this nature arises out of the heavy emphasis on a national approach to the solution of economic problems and the increasing tendency for economists to be employed in national government services with consequent danger that an independent scientific approach may be displaced by a narrow national point of view....These tendencies may be

> counteracted in some measure if, from time to time, economists could be brought together at informal meetings providing an appropriate atmosphere and agenda for scientific discussions.[13]

The Rockefeller Foundation agreed to back this proposition. Accordingly, a conference was convened in Geneva for 8–12 September 1949. The talent among those present was remarkable. The United Kingdom provided the largest delegation: Thomas Balogh, F. A. Burchardt, D. G. Champernowne, J. M. Fleming, Mrs M. F. W. Hemming, Sir Hubert Henderson, Arthur Loveday, G. D. A. MacDougall, E. F. Schumacher, and Piero Sraffa. Italy was represented by Paulo Baffi, F. di Fenizio, and V. Travaglini. Delegates from France were Maurice Bye, Francois Perroux, A. Sauvy, and Pierre Uri. Erik Lundberg and Kjeld Philip came from Sweden. Denmark was represented by Jorgen Gelting, Carl Iverson, and Jorgen Pedersen. Jan Tinbergen came from the Netherlands and Ragnar Frisch from Norway. E. H. Chamberlin and Gottfried Haberler were there from the United States; Karl Brunner and E. Rappard represented Switzerland. Ernst John came from Austria.[14]

Economists from the Eastern bloc were notable for their absence. A number of them were invited: among them, E. S. Varga and K. V. Ostrovitianov (USSR), Ivan Stefanoff (Bulgaria), Ludvik Frejka (Czechoslovakia), and Oskar Lange (Poland).[15] In the end, none of them made it to Geneva, though Lange and Frejka had hoped to be able to do so. As Myrdal noted, 'The absence of economists from Eastern Europe meant, of course, that the topics were mainly discussed from a Western European point of view.' He further reported that opinions on devaluation as a corrective for balance-of-payments difficulties were fairly evenly divided. Though devaluation of the pound sterling (followed by similar action by most other West European governments) occurred only a matter of days after the conference adjourned, 'there was no clear forecast of the event' among those assembled.[16]

Though the conference exercise was not to be repeated, the Rockefeller Foundation continued to support the ECE's work in other ways. From 1948 to 1955, it financed an 'In-service Stipend Scheme' at the ECE for younger economists. Myrdal intended that this program should be aimed at countries where opportunities for postgraduate training were limited, particularly in Eastern Europe. But the cold war made it difficult to recruit candidates from this area. Twenty-seven stipendiaries were awarded under this program, but only two came from Eastern Europe. Poland and Hungary supplied one each, both of them recruited when they were abroad.[17]

The Rockefeller Foundation also funded a major study prepared by the University of Stockholm's Ingvar Svennilson, entitled *Growth and Stagnation in the European Economy*. Begun in 1949, it was published by the ECE in 1954. This highly regarded analysis concentrated particularly on the performance of European economies between 1913 and 1938. Svennilson found that Europe's growth rate between the two world wars fell short of the rate achieved before 1913. In large measure, this outcome could be attributed to its failure to transform its patterns of trade and production in response to the changing structure of the world economy.[18]

Further aspects of the work of the Research and Planning Division

When at full strength, the staff of the Research and Planning Division numbered 63, of whom 35 were professional economists or statisticians. Most of the professionals – within whose ranks a wide variety of nationalities were represented – planned to spend the bulk of their careers in university life and served the ECE for 2 years or so while on leave from their home base. Insofar as possible, a spirit of academic freedom was cultivated in the Division's work environment, subject to the qualification that the studies it conducted should be oriented toward the solution of practical problems. Theorizing for theorizing's sake was not on.

In addition, analysts in the Research Division were encouraged to be hard-hitting – so long as they had the facts to back their position – when they spotted problems in need of attention. When they reported on such issues in the Annual Surveys and other publications, testimony to the truth was to be the guiding criterion: The risk that their findings might offend sensibilities in one or more of the member governments was irrelevant. This did indeed invite some controversies when, for example, France was criticized for tolerating a 'foreign exchange black market' operating in Paris 'during each crisis of confidence'; or when the United Kingdom was taken to task for permitting wasteful inefficiencies in the consumption of coal; or when estimates of the real military budget of the USSR were published. Though initially criticized for its investigations into economic development problems in Southern Europe (especially in Italy and Greece), the Division was later congratulated for breaking new ground in the study of underdevelopment. Activities such as these were possible because the Secretariat insisted that the ECE's studies would not be referred to member governments for 'clearance' prior to publication. Instead the pertinent documents, when completed, would be made available to all simultaneously.[19]

Appraising the achievement

Myrdal was justifiably proud to have built a robust international institution from scratch and to have navigated it successfully through uncharted waters. But he was also acutely conscious of the shortfall between what could have been accomplished and what had actually been achieved. As he put it in the last of his opening statements to a session of the ECE in April 1957, 'The more tightly the limitation of the political factors has affected economic cooperation, the bigger would be the common gains of such cooperation – if it were possible. On an immense scale the cold war holds back economic progress on both sides of the dividing line. Big projects which are not only very useful, but in a more sane political situation would be deemed almost necessary, cannot be undertaken and are not even contemplated as a practical possibility.'[20]

How was this shortfall between possibilities and performance to be understood? There was no escaping the cold war as a factor. But perhaps there were some deeper reasons. Casting himself in the role of a 'participant-observer,' Myrdal sought to probe this matter in three major lectures in the early 1950s. Each of them turned on a conception that increased national integration, a central reality of the past three decades or so in the advanced Western countries, had been accompanied by international disintegration.

The first of these lectures, delivered at the University of Manchester in March 1950, spelled out this characterization of the world situation in some detail. The growth in national integration since the 1930s could be understood as the response of the several governments to circumstances of the Great Depression. To deal with the problems presented by mass unemployment, governments were obliged to intervene in the economy and on an increasing scale. Myrdal saw this as the 'trend towards economic planning.' It meant that *laissez-faire* was genuinely dead and that the various publics would not countenance a return to a regime ordered by the invisible hand. There was no point in lamenting this phenomenon. In his view, 'the price mechanism does not function any longer to restore equilibrium,' adding 'that a free economy under present circumstances is not a very practical proposition.'[21] In the post-World War II political environment, virtually all Western governments had committed themselves to the maintenance of full employment as the overriding imperative of economic policy. This meant that still more governmental intervention in the economy was required. Post-war Europe, he further noted, would need to rely on visible hands to stave off chronic balance-of-payments crises.[22]

Myrdal regarded the trend towards planning as 'non-reversible' and saw it as another example of the principle of 'cumulative causation' at work, with 'international and internal causes in interplay.' On this theme, he wrote,

> On the one hand, the tremendous shocks from outside, the international disequilibria and insecurities, have continuously been putting the individual States under the necessity of ever more State interventions and economic planning. On the other hand, there is no doubt that national economic planning, necessitated or given a spur by international disturbances, in its turn continuously works as an important obstacle to restoring international equilibrium in trade and payments by automatic adjustments within the price mechanism.[23]

The gold standard in its classic form could be regarded as the primary example of an internationalist mechanism, so long as all the players abided by the 'rules of the game.' Its demise was also a signal instance of 'international disintegration.' But no useful purpose would be served by sentimentalizing this phenomenon – the classical gold standard was beyond recovery. It needed to be recognized, however, that the high hopes the internationalists had attached to the Bretton Woods instruments for governing a world monetary order had not been realized. No modern government was prepared to allow its domestic economic policies to be controlled by the state of its international balances.

In his treatment of the 'trend towards economic planning,' Myrdal also drew attention to vulnerabilities arising from the commitment of nation-states to pursue policies of full employment. He envisioned situations in which governments were effectively held hostage by various interest groups. Thus, there was an 'inherent tendency to inflation in our planned economies' that arose from their 'democratic foundation.' He explained its mechanism as follows:

> Where prices and wages are not pure market phenomena any longer but are being regulated, this means . . . that we all, through our own representatives, determine our own and each other's incomes by collective bargaining. It is natural if, in this political process, when we are trying to keep our own remuneration as high as possible, we are tempted to agree to a compromise allowing also other people's incomes to go up.

There was a novel analytic insight here into a process that would later be described as 'rent-seeking' when private pressure groups exploit the political sphere for their own advantage. On this point, Myrdal was ahead of the field by a couple of decades.[24]

Governments, Myrdal advised, should stiffen their resistance to this 'inherent' inflationary tendency by maintaining internal monetary balance. Otherwise, they would be inclined to resort to a 'bad solution' in their attempts to suppress inflation. This would be unfortunate because 'it necessitates a large number of State interventions which have as their sole motivation the need to counteract the too large aggregate nominal incomes: rationing, building controls, allocations, price controls, and so on. This spreading out of State controls into detailed "regimentation" results in all sorts of uneconomic dislocations, hampering production.' It also meant that the 'political and economic brains of the country' would become preoccupied 'by all this petty tampering.' Their energies should instead be focused on long-term economic planning which should begin by balancing aggregate demand and aggregate supply.[25] Myrdal explored some further aspects of the world situation in a 1954 lecture prepared for delivery to the Society for the Psychological Study of Social Issues in the United States. Its focus was signaled by its title – 'Psychological

Impediments to Effective International Cooperation.' He recognized that East–West tensions presented formidable stumbling blocks to cooperation on a world scale. But performance within the Western community had also been disappointing. He could 'testify', he wrote, 'that in the economic field no accomplishment of Western cooperation has as yet broken decisively the general trend of economic international disintegration . . .'[26] For the sake of argument, he wanted to exclude the cold war and its many ramifications from his analysis in order to concentrate on 'psychological factors of an even more permanent and basic nature which would have been present even if the relations between the Soviet Union and the West had come to develop in the way most people, including statesmen, in the Western countries and particularly in America rightly wished but mistakenly expected during the war.'[27]

His line of inquiry could profitably begin by taking note of the differences in the way public attitudes are formed with respect to domestic policies, on the one hand, and toward foreign policies, on the other. Myrdal diagnosed the problem as follows: In the nationally integrated state, 'to an ever larger number of people internal politics takes on a character of having a clear and concrete significance which is commonly understood. This tends to give a sense of relative security.' The matter of foreign policy stood in sharp contrast. 'There is an objective element of uncertainty in foreign policy,' he observed, 'namely the absence of a certain reasonable predictability concerning the consistency of other nations' attitudes and policies which is necessary for confidence to move ahead in cooperation.'[28]

But there were further complications here. People's attitudes were 'immensely more sensitive and unstable, much less calm, realistic and dependable in international than in internal affairs.' And attitudes toward 'the other' were also more subject to manipulation. Myrdal regarded it as 'a sad but accurate commentary on the mental state of humanity today that it is always so much easier to get people to join against something than for something. The foreigner is the obvious choice of an adversary if one wants to use this means to preserve and enhance the unity of the nation.'[29] An additional psychological impediment to improved international cooperation was the 'cultural isolation' to which most of the world's inhabitants were subjected. Growth in tourism provided increased opportunities for exposure to foreign cultures, but this form of contact was likely to be superficial and impressionistic. Genuine cultural understanding, in his view, could best arise from the total immersion that came with living and working in another country. Ironically, this was more difficult to do in the 1950s than it had been a half-century earlier. Before World War I, there had been few barriers to the international migration of labor in Western countries. But, with the modern world's restrictions on labor mobility, this was no longer the case. In their concerns to insure full employment for their own citizens, governments were inclined to take a suspicious view of foreigners as competitors with their own in the labor market.

Despite these obstacles, Myrdal did not altogether abandon hope for improved international cooperation. Admittedly on a modest scale, he had seen it in action in the ECE Secretariat, where a staff of international civil servants had managed to develop an 'internationalist' mentality. He identified a number of factors that had made this possible:

> first, an active recruitment policy which goes after character and competence and systematically avoids government appointees; second, the sustaining of safeguards for the integrity of staff members in the face of national pressures; thirdly, the stimulation of continuous awareness of the larger objectives of the organization; fourthly, the guarding of the Secretariat initiative in the sphere constitutionally provided for it, and the continuous formation of a cautious but clear and firm Secretariat policy.[30]

The third lecture in this sequence was delivered as the L. T. Hobhouse lecture at Bedford College in the University of London on 25 February 1954. Its theme was 'realities and illusions' with regard to the functioning of inter-governmental organizations. This characterization of the organizations in question as 'inter-governmental,' rather than 'international,' was significant. Myrdal's central point was that 'international organizations are nothing less than instruments for the policies of individual governments...'[31] Misunderstandings, he maintained, had arisen because much of the public was not cognizant of this 'reality.' Instead, substantial bodies of opinion continued to entertain the 'illusion' that international organizations created at the end of World War II would manifest the 'one-world' ideal that had been articulated in the flush of Allied victory. All of this presupposed, of course, that the Grand Alliance which had won the war would be sustained in peacetime. When this presupposition was falsified by reality, 'illusion' was transformed into 'disillusion.' If expectations had been tempered by a reading of historical experiences, this disillusion need not have happened.

Speaking to his work at the ECE, Myrdal remarked that he was 'deeply conscious of how almost futile our attempts are when measured in terms of the real possibilities for economic cooperation that exist.' By way of explanation, he re-introduced a familiar argument: 'In the present era of national integration and international disintegration the governments have not been prepared to accept more than a very limited amount of international cooperation even in the economic field.'[32] Nonetheless, there was something worthwhile about the ECE's existence as an institution: It could perform the function of an honest broker. He reported that 'the most important instance within the experience of secretariat brokerage is, of course, the responsibility given the Secretariat in sponsoring multilateral and bilateral East–West trade contacts.'[33]

The Secretariat was authorized to convene off-the-record meetings of trade experts from the various governments, which were known as 'Consultations.' Myrdal assessed this development as follows: 'This new form of inter-governmental cooperation in a particularly difficult field has been found especially useful by governments in avoiding political quandaries which other forms of meeting could not overcome.'[34]

By early 1954 – when these words were written – the thaw in East–West relations that followed the death of Stalin brought the ECE closer to being an all-Europe institution than it had ever been before.

Further studies of the international economy, 1956–1957

Though his duties as Executive Secretary of the ECE continued to keep him busy, Myrdal still managed to produce major works on aspects of international economic issues that extended well beyond Europe. The year 1956 witnessed the publication of a major treatise of some 380 pages entitled *An International Economy: Problems and Prospects*. This work was broad in scope, embracing the whole of the non-Soviet world with particular attention to the relationships between rich countries and poor ones. Myrdal's text included an extended treatment of the phenomenon he had identified earlier in his discussion of the problems stemming from the co-existence of 'national integration and international disintegration.' In this instance, he proposed to examine the prospects of moving the international system from a state of disintegration to one of integration.

As noted earlier, national integration – in which individual governments jealously defended their sovereign jurisdictions over domestic economic policy – was at once responsible for a considerable part of the international disintegration and an obstacle to international re-integration. Put in this way, one might be inclined to conclude that reducing the degree to which nation-states were internally integrated might contribute toward easing the passage toward international re-integration. Such an inference would be totally alien to Myrdal's way of thinking. In his reading of the situation, the ultimate goal of international integration could be solidly grounded only when it rested on the foundation of integrated nation-states that had achieved a confidence and maturity sufficient for them to embrace openly the wider international community.

Myrdal added some specificity to his conception when writing as follows:

> *'Economic integration' is the realization of the old Western ideal of equality of opportunity*. The essential element of this ideal, as we commonly understand it when it is related to social relations within one country, is the loosening of social rigidities which prevent individuals from choosing freely the conditions of their work and life. The economy is not integrated unless all avenues are open to everybody and the remunerations paid for productive services are equal, regardless of racial, social, and cultural differences.

Western nations had not yet arrived at the ideal state of complete equality of opportunity, but redistributional reforms over the past century had brought them a long way toward it. It was now time to move the poorer parts of the world in that direction. Myrdal had no doubts '*that economic integration in this sense – international as well as national – is desirable*' and he identified it as '*the specific value premise of the present study*.'[35] He further noted that if the dream of equality of opportunity could be approximated in reality on a global scale, it would mean that '*the concept of the welfare state, to which we are now giving reality in all the advanced nations, would have to be widened and changed into a concept of a "welfare world"*.'[36] It is one thing to stipulate an objective and quite another to devise the practical measures that might contribute to its realization. There could be no escaping the fact that the task of moving the underdeveloped parts of the world along the path to economic progress would be daunting. He recognized that 'most of the underdeveloped countries have deeply disintegrated national economies' and that this would require major institutional reforms before they would be prepared for development.[37] But the economist who thought seriously about attacking these problems would be obliged to confront another issue, namely the extent to which his conceptual kit – which had, after all, been created to deal with issues in the richer countries – could be satisfactorily applied to the analysis of the poorer ones. That question lay at the heart of debates in the mid-1950s over the distribution of benefits between countries participating in international trade.

It needs to be recalled that the exports of most underdeveloped economies at that time were dominated by primary commodities that were sold competitively on international markets. Meanwhile these countries were heavily dependent on imports from the more advanced economies to meet their needs for manufactured goods. Myrdal saw this state of affairs as a condition of economic imbalance. It was true that all underdeveloped countries perceived a major push toward industrialization as the corrective. But this could not happen if these economies were to follow the 'free trade' rules for international commerce. On this point, Myrdal quoted approvingly Raul Prebisch, a fellow international civil servant who directed the UN's Economic Commission for Latin America. In Prebisch's words,

> there exists an obvious disequilibrium, a fact whatever its explanation or justification, that destroys the basic premise underlying the scheme of the international division of labor. Hence, the fundamental significance of the industrialization of the new countries. Industrialization is not an end in itself, but the principal means at the disposal of those countries of obtaining a share of the benefits of technical progress and of progressively raising the standard of living of the workers.[38]

A push toward industrialization would obviously require substantial resources in foreign exchange. For most of the undeveloped world, export earnings were derived from the sale of agricultural products and raw materials. There were reasons to suspect that the terms of international trade were biased against the poor countries. Certainly Prebisch believed this to be the case. Whereas the poor countries' exports were priced competitively on world markets, prices of the manufactured goods which they imported could be administered in markets that were less than fully competitive. And there was no question that price fluctuations were far more volatile for primary products than for manufactures. Myrdal was sympathetic to this line of argument. To assist the underdeveloped countries in maximizing their foreign exchange earnings, he urged them to join forces in order to strengthen their collective bargaining power.[39]

But industrialization programs also called for much more than this. Protection for nascent industries would be required in order to shelter them from competition from producers in the rich countries whose costs, at least initially, would be considerably lower than those incurred by the 'infant.' And he drew a sharp line of distinction between the principles to guide commercial policies of the poor and the rich. There was a solid rationale, he maintained, for a 'double standard.' When the advanced countries imposed restrictions on imports, the volume of international trade shrank and this was to be lamented. In the case of the underdeveloped countries, trade barriers protecting local industry did not diminish world trade. The constraint affecting their trading behavior was the availability of foreign exchange. Whatever they managed to earn would be spent on capital goods and raw materials needed for an industrialization program. Rationing of foreign exchange by a planning authority would be needed to insure that the most urgent requirements were met. (He referred to this procedure in terms of the magnitude of 'international space' available to a policy-maker. This formulation was reminiscent of his memorandum on Sweden's fiscal policy in 1933 and its treatment of possible limits to an expansionary program.) Maintaining 'international space' in an industrializing poor country meant a change in the commodity composition of imports, but not a reduction in the aggregate volume.[40]

Myrdal concluded this study with the observation that '*in the present stage of history nations in the non-Soviet world are not prepared in peacetime to accept the degree of international human solidarity which would make possible progress towards international economic integration.*'[41] But he remained convinced that the underdeveloped countries should vigorously 'push their interests which, almost by definition, are broadly the interests of international integration. The effort from their side is necessary for progress towards equality of opportunity; for . . . it would be illusory to expect that the advanced nations would accommodate them merely out of their good will.' But there was a possible silver lining here. If they pressed effectively, 'the underprivileged nations will have many to support them in the advanced countries. For their requests will appeal to ideals which are cherished in these countries, even when they are not lived up to.'[42] The last sentence resonates with overtones of an argument that was crucial in the presentation of *An American Dilemma*.

Myrdal reiterated many of these points in a volume based on lectures delivered at Yale University in 1958: The published version was entitled *Beyond the Welfare State*. In his thinking at this point, he envisioned the possibility that the advanced welfare states might have so successfully achieved national integration that the role of the state itself could be reconceptualized. In a future ideal world, he wrote, it would be 'in line with the ideals of the Welfare State to delegate, wherever it is safe and practicable, responsibility for detailed public regulations to local and sectional collective authorities instead of having them carried out by means of direct state intervention.' Thus, 'an actual decrease of state intervention' could be accomplished. This outcome presupposed 'a continuing strengthening of provincial and municipal self-government and a balanced growth of the infra-structure of effective interest organizations' as well as 'intensified citizens' participation . . .'[43] The task of reconciling national integration with international re-integration would remain. He entertained the hope that new inter-governmental organizations could bring this to pass by fostering international cooperation. '. . . (A)fter having been a participant in, and an observer of, this work for ten years, I am more convinced than ever that we are on the right track . . . ' He added, 'If a major war is avoided, I believe that the trend will be for the inter-governmental economic organizations to grow in importance.'[44]

Focusing on the less developed world

At the invitation of the National Bank of Egypt – which had commissioned him to deliver a set of lectures in 1955 – Myrdal directed concentrated attention to the problems confronting the underdeveloped parts of the world. The lectures appeared in published form in 1956 under the title *Development and Underdevelopment: A Note on the Mechanism of National and International Economic Inequality.*[45] In 1957, slightly extended versions of these lectures were published in Britain and in the United States: Their texts were identical, but the titles were different. The British edition was entitled *Economic Theory and Underdeveloped Regions*; the American one, *Rich Lands and Poor*. These studies were organized around the issue of increasing inequalities between the rich and the poor nations and between the rich and the poor regions within nations. Myrdal's inquiry was influenced in considerable measure by the investigations conducted by the ECE in 1953 and 1954 when the Research and Planning Division directed its focus to underdevelopment in Southern Europe, with special attention to the circumstances of the poorer regions of Italy and Greece.

The phenomenon of increasing international and inter-regional inequalities, Myrdal maintained, could not be satisfactorily explained within the framework of orthodox economic theory. After all, its fundamental teachings held that the free play of the market should tend to diminish initial inequalities in income. One thus needed to look elsewhere to gain an understanding of the observable realities. From Myrdal's perspective, standard economic theory – based on expectations that economic disturbances would stimulate adjustments toward a stable equilibrium – had gotten it all wrong. Instead, uninhibited market forces were themselves responsible for magnifying inequalities. When the poor were exposed to the rich in unsheltered competition, the initial disparities would tend to widen because of the working of the principle of cumulative causation. The pattern of change would not tend to eliminate the original competitive disadvantage of the poor country or region, but rather to worsen it. Thus the rich would get richer, and the poor, poorer. An adage that 'nothing succeeds like success' would be validated and Myrdal would add that 'nothing fails like failure.'

Myrdal augmented the economist's vocabulary when examining these mechanisms in greater detail. Poor countries and regions would be disadvantaged in their interaction with the rich because of the 'back-setting effect.' (In 1957 variations on the Cairo lectures, the expression 'backwash effect' was substituted.) Consider, for example, the circumstances of the poor country or region. By virtue of its very poverty, the handicaps of inadequacies in the road system and in public utilities are unlikely to be corrected, leaving the area unattractive to new businesses. Similarly, provisions for educational and health services are likely to be substandard, with the consequence that labor force productivity would be compromised. A happier outcome was, in principle, conceivable. Myrdal discussed it in terms of 'spread effects' that might radiate from the expanding rich country or region to uplift the poorer ones. The expansionary momentum could be expected to create fresh market demands for foodstuffs and raw materials. But, how well positioned was the poorer country or region to respond to this stimulus? The capacity for a favorable response, as Myrdal saw it, was itself a function of the level of development. The more backward the area, the less likely was the prospect that it could readjust its production pattern to seize these opportunities. Given the impediments imposed by poverty, it appeared that – in all too many cases – the 'backwash effects' would swamp the 'spread effects.'

How could this vicious circle be broken? At the national level, Myrdal saw no satisfactory alternative to a regime of national planning that would provide shelter from the vicissitudes of unchecked market forces. One of its central tasks would be to create an industrial base that could provide the dynamic for economic uplift. This necessitated protective shelter from the force of foreign competition. He re-introduced here the arguments that he had worked out in *An International Economy* to demonstrate the 'morality' of a 'double standard' in trade practices. While the advanced countries were urged to reduce barriers to the free flow of international trade, the underdeveloped countries were justified in erecting them. And he remained convinced that '*the road to international integration must go over national integration; nationalistic policies by the poor countries and an increase in their bargaining power, won through these policies and through increased cooperation between them as a group, is a necessary stage towards a more effective world-wide cooperation.*'[46] Myrdal was convinced that rich countries were under a 'moral obligation' to realign their priorities in support of economic uplift in poor ones. He recalled Marx's prediction that the process of industrialization in Western capitalist countries would intensify class conflict to the point of sparking a revolution that would destroy the system. Recent history had discredited that forecast, at least as far as frictions between classes within the rich countries were concerned. But it remained an open question whether or not the polarization between rich and poor countries on the global stage might breed destabilizing violence. It was in everyone's interest to keep that from happening.

Some reactions

Critical responses to Myrdal's diagnosis of the state of the international economy and to his policy prescriptions were mixed. Two ECE veterans welcomed his contributions. Walt Rostow, writing in collaboration with his wife, hailed the publication of *An International Economy* as 'an exercise in the principles of the Enlightenment... [and] a rigorous demonstration that the deepest, most easily forgotten precepts of democratic societies are still relevant and useful... ' For these reasons, the book would 'rank among the foremost works of social science in the twentieth century.'[47] Helen Makower applauded Myrdal's concern 'to bring home to the people of all free countries the dangers they are in and to indicate possible ways of escaping from them.'[48] Kenneth Boulding described *An International Economy* as 'an important and moving piece of work.' He added as follows:

> It is a measure of the stature of this work that one compares it with Adam Smith's *Wealth of Nations*. It has the same breadth of vision, the same passion for human welfare, even occasionally the same poignard of wit. In place of Smith's 'natural liberty', however, we are offered world integration, achieved by discrimination against the rich nations, as national integration is achieved by discrimination against rich individuals.[49]

But the applause was far from universal. Raymond Mikesell, then at the University of Virginia, was outspokenly negative. He challenged Myrdal's reading of 'equality of opportunity,' noting that the extension of governmental control over private enterprise, as advocated by the author, would be regarded by some as a negation of that goal. He expressed doubts about the accuracy of claims that the terms of trade faced by poor countries were, in fact, deteriorating. He described Myrdal's 'sympathy for the aspirations of the poorer countries' as 'deep and commendable,' but it was unfortunate that it had 'led him to apologize for or rationalize excessive nationalism instead of dealing critically with their restrictive and autarkic policies, many of which are dictated more by political favoritism and the protection of the interests of the few rather than by the welfare of the many.' He questioned the wisdom of encouraging underdeveloped nations 'to use any means to promote industrialization, no matter what the implications for a rational distribution of resources or the economic freedom of the people concerned may be.' He concluded that the author had 'perhaps emphasized the political and social factors in the international economy at the expense of rigorous economic analysis.'[50]

All of this served as a prelude to a three-volume study, entitled *Asian Drama: An Inquiry into the Poverty of Nations* – that was to preoccupy Myrdal for the next decade.

Notes

1. G. Myrdal, 'The Research Work of the Secretariat of the Economic Commission for Europe,' *25 Economic Essays in Honour of Erik Lindahl* (Stockholm: Ekonomisk tidskrift, 1956), p. 270.
2. As reported by David Wightman, *Economic Cooperation in Europe: A Study of the United Nations Economic Commission for Europe* (London: Stevens and Sons Ltd and William Heineman Ltd).
3. For background on the formative phases of the ECE, see W. W. Rostow, 'The Economic Commission for Europe,' *International Organization*, 3:2 (May 1949) 254–68. Rostow served on the staff of the ECE Secretariat from its inception until mid-1949.
4. 'ECE's New Deputy Executive Secretary,' *United Nations Bulletin*, 5 (1 October 1948) 772.
5. G. Myrdal, 'Prospects of the Economic Commission for Europe,' *United Nations Weekly Bulletin*, 3 (29 July 1947) 147.
6. Ibid.
7. *United Nations Bulletin*, 4 (1 February 1948).
8. G. Myrdal, op. cit., 149.
9. A. P. Thirlwall, *Nicholas Kaldor* (New York: New York University Press, 1987), pp. 104–05.
10. G. Myrdal, 'The Research Work of the Secretariat of the Economic Commission for Europe,' p. 290.

11. Ibid., pp. 268–69.
12. G. Myrdal, 'Memorandum on proposed periodic conferences of economists to be held in Geneva under the Rockefeller Foundation Project,' 5 November 1948, Rockefeller Foundation Archives, Record Group 1.2, Series 100.
13. Ibid.
14. Ibid.
15. G. Myrdal to N. Buchanan, Rockefeller Foundation, 6 September 1949, Rockefeller Foundation Archives, Record Group 1.2, Series 100.
16. G. Myrdal to N. Buchanan, Rockefeller Foundation, 26 September 1949, Rockefeller Foundation Archives, Record Group 1.2, Series 100.
17. G. Myrdal, 'The Research Work of the Secretariat of the Economic Commission for Europe,' p. 273.
18. 'Growth and Stagnation in Europe's Economy,' *UN Review*, 1 (March 1955) 43–4.
19. R. Girod, 'How the Public Is Told About the Results of Surveys Carried Out by International Organizations,' *UNESCO, International Social Science Bulletin*, 4:4 (1952); and G. Myrdal, op. cit.
20. G. Myrdal, 'Opening Statement by the Executive Secretary to the 12th Session of the United Nations Economic Commission for Europe,' April 1957, as quoted in G. Myrdal, 'Twenty Years of the United Nations Economic Commission for Europe,' *International Organization*, 22 (1968) 625.
21. G. Myrdal, 'The Trend Towards Economic Planning' (transcript of the Ludwig Mond lecture at the University of Manchester, 13 March 1950), *The Manchester School*, 19 (January 1951) 7. In a footnote, Myrdal reported that 'some of the main thoughts' presented here were earlier contained in his inaugural lecture as Professor in the University of Stockholm in 1935.
22. Ibid., 25.
23. Ibid., 32.
24. Ibid., 35.
25. Ibid., 36.
26. G. Myrdal, 'Psychological Impediments to Effective International Cooperation,' *Journal of Social Issues*, Supplemental Series 6 (1952) 9.
27. Ibid., 11.
28. Ibid., 13.
29. Ibid., 15, 16.
30. Ibid., 25.
31. G. Myrdal, 'Realities and Illusions in Regard to Inter-governmental Organizations,' L. T. Hobhouse Memorial Lecture No. 24, Bedford College, London, 25 February 1954, Oxford University Press, London, 1955, 5.
32. Ibid., 18.
33. Ibid., 24.
34. Ibid.
35. G. Myrdal, *An International Economy: Problems and Prospects* (New York: Harper and Brothers, 1956), pp. 11, 12. Italics in the original.

36. Ibid., p. 324. Italics in the original.
37. Ibid., p. 167.
38. R. Prebisch, as quoted by Myrdal in op. cit., p. 226.
39. Ibid., p. 319.
40. Ibid., pp. 274–76, 288.
41. Ibid., p. 315.
42. Ibid., p. 321.
43. G. Myrdal, *Beyond the Welfare State* (New Haven and London: Yale University Press, 1960), p. 93.
44. Ibid., p. 282.
45. See G. Myrdal, Development and Underdevelopment: a Note on the Mechanism of National and International Economic Inequality (Cairo: National Bank of Egypt Fiftieth Anniversary Commemoration Lectures, 1956).
46. Ibid., p. 76. Italics in the original.
47. W. W. and E. Rostow, 'Mr. Myrdal Brings Utilitarianism Up to Date,' *The Reporter*, 5 (12 July 1956) 45.
48. H. Makower, 'Review of "An International Economy,"' *Economica*, 24 (August 1957) 262.
49. K. Boulding, 'Warning to Nineveh,' *The Christian Century*, 73:Pt 2 (12 September 1956), 1053.
50. R. F. Mikesell, 'Review of "An International Economy,"' *American Economic Review*, 46 (December 1956) 1011–16.

9

Asian Drama: An Inquiry into the Poverty of Nations (1968)

As his ECE decade drew to a close, Myrdal solicited American foundations for support for a new and substantial research venture. In his prospectus, he described its objective as follows: to make 'a balanced appraisal of the situation in Southern and South-eastern Asia as it is developing under the influences from outside and from within.... A main emphasis of the study... would be on the [economic] problems of the region as a whole.... (The) economic potentialities will be viewed in their social and political context. Thus the study will necessarily include an analysis of the new nationalism in the region, as it is conditioned by social, cultural, religious and racial conflicts.'[1] This was an extension of the position he had articulated in writings on the prospects for national and international economic 'integration' in the later 1950s. At this juncture, his conception of the projected study directed attention to the way underdeveloped countries in the South Asian region were or were not shaping a self-confident economic nationalism which might ultimately be translated into economic integration internationally. There was a hint here as well that the potentialities for coordinated planning among various South Asian countries would be investigated.

Myrdal encountered more difficulty than he had anticipated when canvassing for funding for this project. The Rockefeller Foundation and the Carnegie Corporation – both of which had been generous to him in the past – declined. So also did the Ford Foundation. His fortunes proved to be much better with the Twentieth Century Fund, based in New York. Its officers awarded him a grant of $140,000 in

1957 (about 10 percent of which would be authorized for Myrdal's salary) for a period of two and a half years. This was then regarded as a reasonable time span for completion of the study.[2]

The scheduling anticipated at the outset proved to be wildly unrealistic. What ultimately appeared as *Asian Drama* – in three volumes with 2284 pages and 16 appendices – was a decade in the making. Moreover, the substantive content of the work departed radically from that which had been originally projected.

The making of *Asian Drama*: Phase I of the exercise

Myrdal embarked on the study accompanied by Ester and Mogens Boserup, a Danish-husband-and-wife team, who were veterans of the Research and Planning Division of the ECE. The first phase involved in-depth field research in the region, with particular attention to India. (The heavy emphasis on India could be justified on grounds that it was by far the largest and most complex of the countries under investigation. But Myrdal had a further personal stake here: Alva had been appointed to head Sweden's Embassy in New Delhi.) In this part of the undertaking, mountains of primary documents were collected. In addition, the Boserups prepared a considerable volume of background memoranda.

In 1961, Myrdal relocated the headquarters of the project to Stockholm. By this time, Alva had been obliged to resign her Ambassadorial post by reason of illness and was under medical treatment in Sweden, and the Boserups – in keeping with their original understanding – had moved on. There was something of a symmetry here between Phase I of this project and the first phase in the preparation of *An American Dilemma*. In both instances, material in abundance had been amassed and, in both, Myrdal was unsure about how to make use of it. In a letter to August Heckscher, President of the Twentieth Century Fund, Myrdal characterized the situation as follows:

> (M)uch of the expenditure for collaborators in the beginning of the work was misspent . . . (The) book developed as a "destiny," diverging from my preconceptions which I now recognize to have been conventional; after the errors and trials the study could certainly have been planned differently, and more economically, but that we could not do at that time.[3]

With regard to the study of the Negro problem in the United States, Myrdal overcame his Phase I perplexities when he hit upon the conception of an 'American dilemma' – in the form of the disjunction between the reigning national ideology and the day-to-day realities in race relations. This provided the organizational thread needed to complete that landmark study. In putting the South Asia project together, there was no comparable epiphany. There was a transformation, however, in the lineup of collaborators.[4]

Stipulation of the value premises informing the work

As of 1961, many aspects of the ultimate direction of the study remained to be determined. But there was absolute clarity in Myrdal's mind about one important dimension of the exercise. In all of his work, he was faithful to the methodological stricture he had articulated in *The Political Element in the Development of Economic Theory*, namely that it was incumbent upon a scholar to state openly the value premises underlying his investigation. In this instance, the core value judgments could be captured under the rubric of the 'modernization ideals.' There was nothing random about this choice. These ideals were compatible with an important dimension of South Asian reality, that is the aspirations of its most enlightened leaders to transform their societies in ways that would support sustained economic and social progress.

Myrdal's specification of the 'modernization ideals' merits elaboration. He identified the following ingredients:

'a. *Rationality*. It is regularly assumed in public debate that policies should be founded on rational considerations.
b. *Development and Planning for Development*. The desire for development and planning for development flows directly from the quest for rationality and represents in the economic and social field the all-embracing and comprehensive expression of the modernization ideals.
c. *Rise of Productivity*. Higher output per head of the population or of the labor force is a commonly shared goal of development planning.

d. *Rise of Levels of Living.* That this valuation is commonly accepted is not surprising in view of the extremely low levels of living of the masses in South Asia.
e. *Social and Economic Equalization.* In all the countries of South Asia the ideal that social and economic stratification should be changed in order to promote equality in status, opportunities, wealth, incomes, and levels of living is commonly accepted in public discussion of the goals for planning and for policies generally.
f. *Improved Institutions and Attitudes.* In general, it is held that social and economic institutions and attitudes should be changed in order to increase labor efficiency and diligence, effective competition, mobility, and enterprise; permit greater equality of opportunities; make possible higher productivity and well-being; and generally promote development.
g. *National Consolidation.* Ideally, national consolidation means a national system of government, courts, and administration that is effective, cohesive, and internally united in purpose and action, with unchallenged authority over all regions and groups within the boundaries of the state.
h. *National Independence.* This ideal is firmly adhered to and, of all the ideals, is given the most explicit expression.
i. *Political Democracy, in a Narrow Sense.* All of the countries of South Asia began their independent existence by declaring their ambition to become democratic nation-states; they gave themselves constitutions, or began to work on constitutions, patterned on those recently evolved in Western countries, with representative assemblies founded on free elections and universal suffrage.
j. *Democracy at the Grass Roots.* Somewhat independent of the political forms and power basis of a national government is the degree to which it is desired that responsibility for their own affairs be delegated to local and sectional communities and accepted by the people in those smaller communities.
k. *Social Discipline versus 'Democratic Planning.'* These communities are all 'soft states,' both in that policies decided on are often not enforced, if they are enacted at all, and in that the authorities, even when framing policies, are reluctant to place obligations on people.'[5]

This formulation of the 'modernization ideals' might be thought of as bearing a functional resemblance to the values embodied in the 'American creed,' as presented in *An American Dilemma*. In both instances, the conceptual apparatus offered a vision of ideal conditions. But there was a fundamental difference. In the 1944 volume, the discrepancy between the ideals of equality and equal justice for all as a practical matter became the driving force behind the momentum for constructive social change. This was possible in the American case – as Myrdal had taken great pains to argue – because virtually all Americans deferred to the principles articulated in the 'creed,' however distant from them their actual behavior might be. There was nothing comparable in the circumstances of South Asian countries. The rank and file in their populations did not identify with the 'modernization ideals.' The overwhelming bulk of the peoples of the region drew their livelihoods from the practice of traditional peasant agriculture. The social environment they inhabited tended to be dominated by attitudes and institutions unreceptive to progressive change. If anything, the experience of the colonial era had hardened resistance to 'modernization.' The techniques of indirect rule deployed by the colonial authorities called for minimal interference in traditional institutions and cultural practices. Moreover, in a number of countries, resistance movements organized to oppose colonial rule had tended to romanticize traditional culture.

These considerations suggested that enthusiasms for 'modernization' among the governing elites were likely to be swamped either by apathy or active opposition on the part of the traditionalists. The weight of the latter in the total population was simply too large. In principle and over time, it was conceivable that traditional attitudes and institutions could be changed by a massive educational effort mounted by the modernizers. But the talents and resources necessary to produce that outcome were not in sight, at least in the near term. In addition, matters were likely to be aggravated by population growth in increments too great to be absorbed in a 'modernizing' sector, even as it grew. Altogether, the forces at work indicated that prospects for a successful realization of the 'modernization ideals' were decidedly gloomy. This train of thought left a mark on Myrdal's psyche. He had been able to survive exposure to some horrifying practices in the American South in the late 1930s and early 1940s because of his conviction that prospects for significant improvement in the plight of the Negro were solid. There was no analogous basis for optimism in the ultimate outcome in the circumstances of the South Asian countries, as he then understood them.

But this was by no means the end of the difficulties. Myrdal's initial intent – as reflected in the arguments of *An International Economy* – was to point the direction in which the policies of South Asian governments should aim in promoting changes that would ultimately position them as first-class members of the international economic community. His hands-on exposure to the realities of the region, however, led him to conclude that this objective – however admirable in principle – was out of reach. This U-turn in his thinking can be accounted for by two primary considerations. The first was his diagnosis of the phenomenon of the 'soft state.' (This usage was one of a number of creative terminological innovations in *Asian Drama*.) This amounted to a recognition that the governments of the region lacked the means or the will to conduct the significant interventions required for the realization of the 'modernization ideals.' By definition, effective planning in the Western (and, more particularly, Scandinavian) countries presupposed that governments could proscribe certain behaviors and encourage others, and with effect. And it was further presupposed that the population generally would recognize governmental authority and support the imposition of penalties to enforce its stipulations. In the West, this kind of discipline was largely taken for granted and it extended over a broad range – for example, from the enforcement of speed limits on highways, to prohibitions on the employment of child labor, to the regulation of health and safety practices in workplaces, and so on. Similar conditions did not prevail in the 'soft states' of the region. For the most part, governments chose not to interfere with many behaviors that were antithetical to a modernizer's conception of rationality – for example, the tolerance in India of superannuated and unproductive cows that represented both an unnecessary claim on resources and a hazard to road users; the refusal of workers in various countries to share space with those who had differing religious, caste, or status identifications. But, even when governments did initiate policies in the interest of 'modernization,' their capacity to implement them was constrained by the scarcity of competent personnel.

Myrdal's pessimism was influenced as well by a second point of contrast between typical practice in advanced countries and that to be found in countries of the region. Corruption of public officials was obviously at odds with the efficient allocation of resources called for in efforts to plan for development. It was acknowledged that this blight was part of the history of the now advanced countries in their earlier stages, though at least the most egregious abuses there had been brought under control by the latter third of the twentieth century. Quantification of the precise magnitude of corruption in South Asia was elusive, but there could be little doubt that it carried heavy weight in determining who got what and when. Myrdal, it should be emphasized, was well ahead of most colleagues in the economics profession in addressing this issue head-on. In general, development economists shied away from this matter, either on grounds that its magnitude could not be reliably determined or because they regarded it as diplomatically impolite to discuss it. *Asian Drama*, on the other hand, highlighted the problem of corruption, even though it contributed to the erosion of the author's initial faith in the promise of uplift through economic planning in the region.

Myrdal's daughter, Sissela Bok, has recorded her father's own report on his mood at the time: 'I used to wake in the middle of the night and think with horror and fear: what in hell am I doing and when will it ever be ready? Writing a book like that is like standing in the trenches of the First World War up to your knees in mud.'[6] Though there appeared to be no grounds for a happy ending to this story, Myrdal did not totally abandon the search for one. This attitude accounts, in considerable measure, for the book's prolonged gestation period. In 1966, for example, he again felt compelled to apologize to the project's sponsors for the further delay in its completion. He could not, he insisted, be faulted for lack of effort: 'I have been laboring harder than at any time of my life and harder than anyone I have seen, in order to get this tremendous work out of my system: days and evenings, Saturdays and Sundays, without vacations.'[7]

Mid-course adjustment: a focus on conceptual criticism

In the Preface to *Asian Drama*, Myrdal explained how and why the final product diverged significantly from what had originally been intended. '(A)s I worked on,' he wrote,

> I became increasingly aware that many of the concepts and theories commonly used in analyzing the problems of the underdeveloped countries in South Asia broke down when scrutinized from the point of view of their logical consistency and their realism, that is, their adequacy to reality. To work my way through what I gradually came to view as severely biased preconceptions – many of which I had shared with most of my fellow economists – was again a slow and painful process.[8]

He added that

> the work on the study became to me personally a destiny, the course of which I had not foreseen or planned from the beginning. I sincerely believe that at the present stage an important contribution to the advance of knowledge about these countries is the negative act of destroying concepts that we had rapidly put together and exposing to criticism masses of more or less worthless statistics collected within the framework of these constructs[9]

He further reported that he was 'deeply conscious of the fact that I have myself shared many of the ways of thought that I criticize in this book.'[10]

Thus the core argument of the three volumes was shaped. It amounted to a sustained attack on the 'transference of Western concepts and theories' to the analysis of the environment of underdeveloped countries such as those found in South Asia. There was little mystery about how this difficulty had arisen. Western economic theorists in the mainstream were inclined to regard their discipline as capable of generating findings with universal validity across time and space. In this mind-set, it was heretical to suggest that the conceptual kit tailored to fit conditions in the advanced countries would not be well suited to grappling with problems of underdeveloped ones, even though they were organized around economic and social structures that stood in fundamental contrast with those typical in Western countries. Myrdal insisted that the fallacies imbedded in this misplaced transference needed to be exposed. This became the primary task of *Asian Drama*. As preliminaries, Myrdal offered a number of examples of Western analytic concepts that did not travel well:

The concepts and the theory of unemployment and underemployment rest on assumptions about attitudes and institutions that, though fairly realistic in the developed countries, are unrealistic in the underdeveloped countries. The neat division of income into two parts, consumption and saving, is realistic in Western societies where the general levels of income and a stratified system of income redistribution by social security policies and other means have largely abrogated any influence of consumption on productivity. This is not the case in underdeveloped countries.

Marx's assumption, so widely adopted by Western economists, that the effects of industrialization and, indeed, of investment generally spread quickly to other sectors of the economy and to institutions and attitudes, may be fairly realistic for Western countries. But as these 'spread effects' are a function of the level of living and of the general culture, the assumption is not valid for most underdeveloped economies, particularly when the sectors of change are small in comparison with the total community.

The lack of mobility and the imperfection of markets in underdeveloped countries rob the analytic method of aggregation of magnitudes – employment, savings, investment, and output – of much of its meaning.[11]

Conceptual critiques: illustrative examples

The theme of misguided transference of Western analytic constructs to the economic environment of South Asia runs throughout the three volumes of *Asian Drama*. Two examples will illustrate the fundamental nature of that criticism. Both are significant in the discourse on economic prospects of the region and in the policy framework within which it was conducted. The first concerns interpretation of underemployment of labor in South Asian countries. The second examines properties of a macro-economic growth model deployed in planning by South Asian governments.

Concepts of unemployment and underemployment – as interpreted in Western countries and in South Asia – called for special attention because of the prevalence of a view that the traditional sectors, based primarily on peasant agriculture, contained a reservoir of labor that could be transferred to urban industrial jobs at minimal cost and with substantial social and economic benefit. One version of this doctrine held that the marginal product of labor in traditional agriculture was negative. This implied that agricultural output would actually rise with the removal of marginal workers. It further suggested that a high priority of policy should be assigned to an industrialization drive that would absorb redundant workers from traditional agriculture.[12]

The proposition that the traditional sector was characterized by some form of labor surplus contrasted sharply with the view predominant during the colonial period. Potential employers of wage laborers – most of whom were then Europeans – regularly complained about shortage of labor. Expatriate owners of plantations and mines (the activities that attracted foreign investors to the region) did indeed experience difficulties in recruiting and retaining local workers. (It needs to be added that they did not experiment by offering substantial increases in wage rates to determine what the supply response would be.) In any event, the world they observed did not exhibit signs that a massive flow of underemployed peasants would take up wage employment if the opportunity presented itself.

It needs to be recalled that a concept of underemployment in the West was originally formulated to speak to a phenomenon observable during the Great Depression. The issue in question concerned the plight of skilled workers who had been laid off from their regular jobs. In an attempt to eke out a livelihood superior to the dole, many of them took up menial tasks that fell well short of utilizing their productive potential. Because they were still active participants in the labor force, they were not treated as unemployed. (The unemployment category was reserved for those who were involuntarily idle.) Instead their situation could be described as one of underemployment because much of their productive potential was wasted for reasons not of their choosing. (The term 'disguised unemployment' was also used as a synonym.) Once the economy recovered, the underemployed would quite readily take up work more commensurate with their skills. These circumstances were worlds removed from the type of underemployment that allegedly prevailed in peasant agriculture.

The fact that labor was underutilized in the traditional sector of South Asian economies was not in dispute. Considerable slack was imbedded therein. But could that slack be usefully analyzed within the framework constructed for labor force analysis in Western countries? There were valid grounds for skepticism on that point.

Entrenched habits of work in peasant agriculture were often accepted as the norm: The presence of substantial idleness was thus tolerated. From the perspective of an external observer, this idleness might be interpreted as waste of potentially productive resources. But peasant farmers had not been forced into this situation involuntarily; for that matter, the issue of choice was not relevant. Some idleness was built into the seasonality of farming activities. Labor inputs might be intense in the planting and harvesting seasons, but slack in other seasons of the farming year could be welcomed as compensation. Perhaps a more serious shortfall in labor input was rooted in the cultural environment. Socially sanctioned taboos on work (or work of particular types) – whether on account of gender, religion, caste, or class – accounted for substantial non-participation in productive activity on the part of many who would otherwise be qualified to perform it. This form of 'underemployment' – perhaps better described as underutilization of labor – was distinctly different from the phenomenon described by this term in Western societies. In traditional societies, it was taken as a given within their structural frameworks.

It should be further noted that this slack did not lend itself to ready mobilization for outward transfer to a modernizing industrial base. Models built around the premise that surplus labor in considerable volume would be available for such a project were out of touch with the structural realities on the ground. They also were in error when suggesting that an exercise of this sort would be essentially costless. Labor transfers of the type called for could be productive only after those exiting the traditional sector had been trained to master the skills and disciplines required in an unfamiliar setting. This was a far cry from the experience of the underemployed in the West during the Great Depression. Their skills could quickly be reactivated, once a demand for their services was present.

Misguided application of conceptual tools devised to address conditions in advanced countries could also be detected in the central planning operations of most South Asian countries. It took the form of the appropriation of post-Keynesian growth models of the Harrod–Domar variety. This type of macro-economic modeling had been devised for the purpose of specifying properties of a growth rate needed to sustain full employment through time. The equilibrium condition required that the increment in aggregate supply created by new investment be matched by an increment in aggregate demand. What fell out of this exercise was a demonstration that the growth rate was determined by the ratio of aggregate saving to aggregate income, divided by a capital coefficient (or capital–output ratio) that reflected the amount of new output created per unit of investment. Modeling of this type was on the cutting edge of macro-economic theorizing in the West in the years immediately following World War II.[13]

It is no wonder that governments of newly independent countries in South Asia should find such an approach to analyzing an economy's growth rate to be appealing. They were inclined to believe that their historical experience entitled them to the best from the West. The latest analytic findings produced there had a compelling aura of technical sophistication. And – at least at a superficial level – the concepts deployed in Harrod–Domar growth models seemed to be addressed to their needs. Thus, it was possible to specify a target rate of growth and to determine what had to happen to achieve it. This exercise, of course, had to be fleshed out with values assigned to the capital–output and saving–income ratios. Reliable empirical data on these magnitudes were not easy to obtain. There was a tendency, however, to adopt a convention used in a number of Western countries, namely to presuppose that the normal value of the capital–output ratio in fully employed economies was 3 (though it would obviously vary considerably in abnormal circumstances, such as wars and depressions). Assigning a numerical evaluation to the saving–income ratio posed a different problem. It was usually posited – and rightly – that the poverty of South Asian countries precluded the achievement of saving–income ratios compatible with their desired rates of growth. A hypothetical example will illustrate the procedure. Suppose that a 5 percent rate of growth in aggregate output is sought. With a capital–output ratio valued at 3, the ratio of aggregate saving to aggregate income would need to be 15 percent. It might reasonably be concluded that domestic saving on this scale in a poor country was not achievable, but that a decidedly lower rate – say, 5 percent – was within reach. A South Asian government could then solicit advanced countries for support – through grants, loans, and direct investment – to cover the shortfall in saving at home. Favorable responses of the indicated scale should enable it to realize the growth rate to which it aspired. A growth model of the Harrod–Domar variety clearly had its uses (or abuses).

But how well suited were these analytic constructs to the South Asian environment? Consider, for example, the concept of an aggregate capital–output ratio. Even in advanced countries, its precise magnitude was difficult to determine: There was more than a touch of arbitrariness in the conventional valuation at 3. One could, however, be reasonably confident that there was some fairly predictable relationship between an increment in the capital stock and a subsequent increase in output, even though quantitative exactness in this regard might be elusive. When new investments were put in place, one had every reason to expect that workers with the right skills to use the new tools would be available, along with competent managers. In the West, there was typically little worry as well about the adequacy of a supporting infrastructure: for example, transport and communication facilities, and power supplies. In South Asian economies, there was no basis for similar confidence. In their societies, lots of other things needed to happen – things that might very well be resisted within the framework of prevailing institutions and attitudes – before an addition to capital could be translated into enlarged outputs.

The assimilation of a Harrod–Domar mentality into economic thinking in South Asia was mischievous for another reason. It had the effect of emphasizing one factor, to the exclusion of all others – namely capital formation – as the propelling force driving a nation's economic growth. Meanwhile, it systematically diverted attention away from other relevant matters. Indeed, the distinctive properties of South Asian societies – particularly the impact of cultural obstacles impeding their growth prospects – were air-brushed out of the picture. With these aspects of the reality factored back in, a reasonably stable and predictable connection between growth in capital and growth in output is lacking. One can certainly conceive of situations in which substantial increases in output can be achieved without new capital formation, as well as cases in which expansion in the aggregate capital stock was not accompanied by enlarged output. In India, for example – with roughly three-quarters of the population engaged in agricultural pursuits – a favorable monsoon can swell aggregate output (and an unfavorable one can diminish it), quite independent of what is happening to the aggregate size of the capital stock.

But there are difficulties as well with the transfer of the Western concept of an aggregate saving–income ratio to South Asia. The Harrod–Domar construct presupposes that saving will be channeled into output-enlarging investment. It further presupposes that the act of saving requires abstention from current consumption. The latter proposition is especially problematic in poor countries which could provide only extremely low levels of living for a substantial segment of the population. In such circumstances, saving that requires reduction in consumption may very well result in shrinkages of total output. This can come about because lowered consumption can have negative effects on nutrition, health, and vitality and, in turn, on work performance and productivity.

An institutional approach

As we have seen, Myrdal's engagement with South Asian realities had led him to reject the approaches to the economic development process offered by mainstream economics. In all too many instances, standard theorizing at the time was contaminated by preconceptions that could not be appropriately fitted to the conditions of the region. This part of the argument of *Asian Drama* had a negative tonality, though Myrdal preferred to think of it as a necessary conceptual cleansing. But where should new analytic moorings be sought? He issued a plea for an institutional approach that would be purged of preconceived conceptual blinders and that would grapple with the facts. In the Prologue, he explained what this approach involved. 'It is not an indulgence in "loose thinking,"' he wrote,

> as some of the conventional economists would be apt to think; on the contrary, it imposes the demand that theories and concepts be logically consistent as well as adequate to reality.... Neither can an institutional approach be characterized as reasoning in 'qualitative terms.' If anything, this approach induces the institutional economist to press harder for research that can give quantitative precision to his theories and bring them to the empirical test.... The goal must always be to quantity facts and the relationships between facts.... Moreover, the institutionalist, since he is basically more critical than the conventional economist, regularly finds the latter's claims to quantitative precision to be unwarranted, often on logical grounds.[14]

In the early stages of his career – in the 1920s and early 1930s – the youthful Myrdal could not have written those sentences. He was then hostile to what he understood an institutional economics to be, and did indeed denounce it as antitheoretical and for encouraging loose thinking.

In large measure, the institutional approach accounts for the bulkiness of the three volumes of *Asian Drama*. As was the case with *An American Dilemma*, there was an encyclopedic dimension. This was part of the mandate to expose the facts and to set them in their appropriate historical, political, and cultural contexts. Thus, there were extended treatments of the colonial experience in various parts of the region and on the way independence movements affected the thinking of those who were to run newly independent governments. The text provides an inventory of the natural resources of the region and their effect on economic activity – past, present, and prospective. There are extended discussions of demographic evolution and its prospects, accompanied by data on resources allocated to health and education programs to improve population quality.

The institutional approach can be seen at work most clearly in the chapters devoted to the discussion of labor utilization in the region. This amounts to an attempt to strip away Western preconceptions regarding labor force analysis and to indicate the manner in which an institutionalist's way of looking at matters can raise a fresh set of questions. In all too many instances, the empirical data needed to give definitive answers to those questions were either lacking or imperfect. But at least this procedure offers an alternative analytic framework to guide further research in the interests of generating a richer understanding of the realities.

The conception of labor utilization presented here can be broken down into three components. The first is that of a participation ratio; that is, the number of people at work at some point of the year in relation to the size of the total population. The most important point to note here is the contrast between conditions in the region and those typical in Western countries. As defined, the participation ratio is considerably higher in South Asia than in the advanced countries. This follows from the quite different behaviors of the very young and very old in these environments. In the advanced countries, eligible participants in the labor force are typically bounded by the age ranges of 16–65 and 16–70. This is the resultant of a number of factors: among them, mandatory requirements for school attendance, legislation proscribing child labor, state-sponsored pension systems, mandatory dates for retirement, and so on. There is no counterpart to these arrangements in South Asia. In traditional agriculture, children at tender ages are labor force participants with duties such as caring for animals. Moreover, the lack of comprehensive educational opportunities minimizes the impact of this form of competition with household work. In the absence of a formalized social security system (beyond that of the extended family), the elderly may remain participants for longer than would be the case otherwise. This approach also invites inspection of those who are not participants and the reasons for their behavior: for example, the bans imposed by gender, religion, and caste; the ranks of the 'educated unemployed' who regard anything but white-collar work as beneath their dignity.

Thinking about labor utilization also calls for inspection of two additional aspects of the overall picture: duration of work time (that is, the number of hours per day and days per year of labor input) and the efficiency of labor input. Typically, the values of these components are lower than would be the case in the West. In a highly organized advanced economy – in which the bulk of labor force participants are employees – the duration of work is reasonably well standardized by the employer's terms of engagement, and is subject to government regulations on, say, the maximum length of the workweek. These conditions are replicated only in small segments of South Asian economies. Instead, the bulk of the active labor force is engaged in activities headed by a self-employed head of household – either in traditional agriculture or in an informal sector in more urbanized areas.

Consider, for example, the typical situation in rural villages. Though there are many variations on this theme throughout the region, the standard pattern of village life is organized around larger landowners at the top of the pyramid and the landless workers at the bottom. In between are the peasants, some of whom own the plots they till, while many others are share-cropping tenants. Given attitudes deeply imbedded in the culture, this environment does not lend itself to effective utilization of labor. Withdrawal from active work conveys high social status and those who can afford it do so. This type of behavior is characteristic of the larger landowners – many of whom are absentees – who can live as rent collectors. Meanwhile, physical labor is stigmatized.

The difficulty with this system is not simply a matter of reduced labor force participation. Share-cropping – in which the gross product is usually split 50–50 between tenant and landlord – significantly compromises the efficiency with which labor is applied.

The tenant who has no security of tenure is deterred from making output-increasing improvements. He is aware that the landlord, not he, can reap the bulk of the benefits. The result is that farm output suffers.

Consider also the nature of labor utilization in the informal sector outside the rural areas. This category embraces a considerable range of activities – for example, petty retailing, rickshaw and taxi services, laundry and cleaning services, garbage collection and disposal, production of some light consumer goods, and – in some instances – building and construction. The informal sector is notable for its ease of entry which permits it to become the sponge for workers who lack other opportunities. Participation ratios here may be high, as is the duration of the workday, month, and year. But the efficiency with which work is performed tends to be low. Issues of this sort are not effectively captured in the conceptual kit developed in Western countries for the study of problems of employment and unemployment.

A framework for thinking about economic policy

From the first phase of the study, an arresting conclusion emerged: that growth in the modern industrial sectors of these economies, even when carried out at the highest feasible pace, would be unable to create enough jobs to absorb the increment in the labor force over the near to medium term. Over the longer term, population growth might well fall – especially if governments carried through plans to promote family planning – and expansion in the number of industrial jobs might accelerate. But the immediate prospect was one in which the creation of non-agricultural jobs would be insufficient to provide placements for a labor force expanded by those already born. Yet another consideration framed the context for discussion of goals for economic policy – a shortfall in the cadres of talented and incorruptible civil servants to administer ambitious programs.

Myrdal's bearishness about job creation in the industrial sector did not mean that industrialization should not be pursued. It should still be pushed, but one needed to be realistic about what it could and could not achieve. When surveying the prospects for industrial growth, he was doubtful about the capacity of newly created industries to break into export markets. This would be desirable, but it was unlikely to be do-able. High start-up costs associated with getting new manufacturers going was likely to compromise their competitiveness in international markets. It was more promising to look to import substitution as a strategy for expanding the industrial base. The outputs that found a market at home could be readily identified by inspecting the established patterns of domestic demand. Implementing this strategy would, however, require protection from the competition of foreign producers. In these circumstances, Myrdal was prepared to endorse protective shelter as needed. He reiterated the arguments he had made on this point in *An International Economy*.

Expanding an industrial base in this manner promised to get some momentum going. At least potentially, this could generate further expansion. In this discussion, he re-introduced a concept that had appeared in his earlier writings – that of 'spread effects.' Additional stimuli, in principle, could be expected when new enterprises generated a new demand for raw materials and other inputs. At the same time, the incomes paid out to workers in the new enterprises would provide a further stimulant to demand. But Myrdal cautioned against expecting too much from the 'spread effects' in the South Asian environment. For some time, he anticipated that these effects would be weak 'as a by-product of the low level of development... and the fact that "elasticity of supply" is, as a result, "low." Stimuli for expansion are soon checked by bottlenecks that reduce the potential spread effects at an early stage. The more important of the barriers to effective and sustained spread can easily be catalogued: deficiencies in the supply of technical administrative personnel, inadequacies in the supply and mobility of skilled labor, bottlenecks in the availability of raw materials and semi-manufactured goods, and deficiencies in transport and power systems.'[15] It was the task of policy-makers to attempt to break such bottlenecks. Eventually, these problems could be solved, but it would take time.

Analyzing the impact of industrialization further called for a look at its 'backwash effects' – that is, the extent to which the outputs of new factories pre-empted the market space previously occupied by other domestic producers, at the cost of income and employment. This concern centered on the fate of the traditional craftsmen who produced a considerable range of the consumer goods and, most importantly, textiles. A substantial case could be made for steering the commodity pattern of the modern factory sector away from products that would compete directly with the traditional crafts. Myrdal put it this way: 'In the villages there is no alternative employment for most of the craftsmen, and the only possible way to improve their lot and, indeed, prevent a further deterioration in their living levels is to give them as much market protection as possible, and at the same time improve their productivity.'[16]

Shaping policy for traditional agriculture posed a still greater challenge. It was easier to stipulate the dimensions of the problem than to solve it. As was noted earlier, this sector of the economy was characterized by underutilization of labor in substantial volume. But this phenomenon was not going to go away – as had been argued in one strand of conventional theorizing – by shifting labor allegedly in surplus to an expanding industrial sector. To the contrary, the limited absorptive capacity of modernizing industry in the near and medium term meant that the traditional agricultural sector would be called upon to provide a berth for more people, rather than fewer. What needed to happen – though there certainly was no guarantee that it would – was that slack would be reduced, while at the same time providing productive space for more workers.

One could point to the direction in which solutions should be sought. The adoption of new farming techniques that raised yields was a paramount objective. Increased use of commercial fertilizers, the introduction of higher-yielding and disease-resisting seeds, extension of irrigation to permit multiple crop cycles in the agricultural year – all of these steps would enhance labor utilization and yield benefits that raised the level of living. A major program in agricultural re-education would be needed to accomplish this. And it would need to be accompanied by significant reforms in established institutions and practices. Among them, credit should be made available on reasonable terms to free farmers from the extortionate clutches of the village moneylender. Improvements in the rural transport system would be required to assure access to markets for increases in total production that were to be hoped for. Above all, the cultivating peasantry needed to be taught how to take advantage of new opportunities and persuaded that it was worthwhile to do so.

This was a tall order – especially in light of what Myrdal recognized to be an 'important constraint' – namely 'the severely limited supply of technical competence available for guiding and directing agricultural production along progressive lines.'[17] It had been his hope that the 'traditional status hierarchies' – between landlord and tenant, between cultivating peasant and landless laborers – could be broken down through land reforms that would move the agricultural sector in the direction of equality. He regarded persistence of these hierarchies as 'an important factor blocking a fuller utilization of labor.' But, somewhat reluctantly, he concluded that because 'neither the political will nor the administrative resources are available for a radical, or for that matter, any fairly effective land reform – it may be preferable to make a deliberate policy choice in favor of capitalist farming by allowing and encouraging the progressive cultivator to reap the full rewards of his enterprise and labor...' This policy recommendation, he insisted, was not a surrender to *laissez-faire*. Instead it called for a major transformation in the *status quo*. The goal should be to reward the productive – in particular, progressive cultivators who were prepared to embrace innovations – and to punish the non-productive. The latter were the absentee landlords and the non-cultivating landowners who should be made subject to severe tax penalties.[18] He did propose one redistributional initiative: an allocation of small plots of unoccupied land to the landless. This was not expected to add significantly to agricultural output. It was intended instead to provide the landless with a modicum of dignity.

Throughout his discussion of economic policies, Myrdal insisted that it was up to the countries of the region themselves to improve their condition. They should not premise their policy-making on the assumption that assistance from foreign aid would do the job for them.

The initial reception in the West

Asian Drama was published in March 1968. Among economists, reviews spanned a considerable spectrum. Thomas (Lord) Balogh of Oxford – whose sympathetic credentials toward unconventional approaches to economic issues were well on record – was lavish in his praise. Writing in the *New York Times Book Review*, he hailed the work as one of two 'massive peaks of interpretative political economy [that] tower over the arid, flat plain inhabited by the conventional modern economists who, lured on by the magic of mathematical determinacy, undue generalization, illicit aggregation, and inadequately documented secular vistas, aspire to the status of scientists.' (The second 'massive peak' was John Kenneth Galbraith's *New Industrial Society*.)[19] Kenneth E. Boulding, President of the American Economic Association, described Myrdal as perhaps 'the world's top social scientist' and welcomed the work. He spoke approvingly of the 'unsparing... criticism of those Western economists and social scientists who think that development is equivalent to technology and who are unable to recognize the obstacles created by ancient tradition, class structures and especially by the existing power structure of society. This is a point which is so underplayed in most Western and especially American writing on the subject that it is refreshing... ' Though he understood what Myrdal meant when speaking about 'soft states' – that is, the absence of disciplines to insure that government policies were carried out – he drew attention to the fact that, in some respects, these states were anything but soft in their treatment of racial minorities: for example, Ceylon (now Sri Lanka) to the Tamils, India to Moslems, Pakistan to Hindus, Indonesia to the Chinese, Burma (now Myanmar) to Indians. Overall, he concluded that the 'insistence on the crucial importance of agriculture, and on the fact that for at least a generation to come no conceivable amount of industrialization will take care of the rapidly growing labor force, shows a very solid quantitative sense of what is perhaps the hardest fact of the whole problem.'[20]

Writing in the *American Economic Review*, George Rosen (then with the Asia Development Bank) regarded Myrdal's criticisms of the use of Western models and concepts in South Asia as 'worth making,' but added that 'in his stress on the need for a more institutional analysis... he himself uses traditional economic concepts centering about the market and the price system as the basis for his own policy suggestions.' Rosen thought the prognosis to be 'gloomier... than justified.' He drew attention to prospects for increasing exports and 'increases in farm output with new technologies, especially with new varieties of seed...,' and noted that 'some of these technological breakthroughs have only begun to have their effects since the book went to press in 1966.'[21] Hla Myint, a development economist at the London School of Economics, observed that the book did not adequately characterize 'the very significant differences between the large and densely populated countries like India and Pakistan and the smaller and less densely populated countries of South-east Asia,' but that the book 'made a major contribution to the understanding of Indian economics.' He further commented, 'Many economists before him have criticised the notion of "disguised unemployment," but Myrdal has developed the attack more systematically by a useful analysis in terms of labour participation, labour duration, and labour efficiency.'[22] The remarks of an American commentator who addressed a general audience deserve also to be reported. John Fischer, editor of *Harper's Magazine*, maintained that 'the main thrust of Myrdal's argument is undeniable' and that, with this book, Myrdal was capable of changing the course of history for a second time.[23]

Enthusiasm for the work, however, was far from universal. P. T. Bauer of the London School of Economics spoke for the school of economists suspicious of government interventions and of non-market solutions to economic problems. 'Even more than other writers on development,' he wrote, 'Professor Myrdal regards material progress, including apparently the transformation of values and conduct, as dependent on state action. The defects of this approach are even more pronounced in the underdeveloped world than elsewhere. In these countries, far more than in the West, the government is primarily a sectional interest.' Bauer concluded,

> The verdict on this book, which is in effect a giant pamphlet, is, therefore, relatively straightforward. Much of it is well worth reading, some parts for their own merit, much larger parts because they show the intellectual results of the paramountcy of politics, the pursuit of political ends rather than a disciplined search for truth, as the aims of social study.[24]

Gustav F. Papanek, based at Harvard's Center for International Studies, also struck a negative note. He attacked particularly what he saw as 'the cavalier neglect of numbers.' Statements to the effect that peasants in South Asia failed to respond to price signals in a manner analogous to the response of farmers in the West called for qualification and quantification. Attention needed to be paid to studies in India and Pakistan, for example, indicating that farmers did 'shift to more lucrative crops even if these crops require more work.'[25] A more sweeping critique came from the pen of an anonymous commentator in the *Times Literary Supplement* of London. The author observed as follows:

> If greatness could be conferred on a book by the time and resources consumed in its composition, there would be no doubt about the answer. It has taken over ten years to produce, has been financed on a scale that only an American foundation can encompass (the figure of over a quarter of a million has been mentioned), and is the result of formidable effort.

In the reviewer's judgment, 'the fundamental weakness in Professor Myrdal's approach . . . is his obsession with the alleged need to *smash through* the obstacles standing in the way of economic growth. . . . (H)e hardly ever considers the possibility of circumventing them, and never does he find himself wondering whether "obsolete" institutions and attitudes might in some cases be actually employed as instruments of progress.'[26] This theme was developed still more forcefully in an extended essay by Clifford Geertz of the anthropology department of the University of Chicago. With particular reference to India – a 'country with so rich a history, so profound a culture, and so complex a social system' – he faulted the study for failing to come adequately to grips with the 'force of its originality and the vitality of its spirit.' 'The civilization that looks to Myrdal to be drifting aimlessly in a sea of anachronisms,' he wrote, 'is actually undergoing the greatest series of changes in its history.' Geertz acknowledged that many things were 'deeply wrong' with Indian institutions – 'with share tenancy, with purdah, with Brahminism, with caste, and with the quality of thought in Indian cafes – and there is no doubt that they must be fundamentally reformed. But such reform must begin with a realization that far from being simple irrationalities, they and the values imbedded in them are responsive to one of the most critical developmental necessities of India: They tend to keep people outside the labor force but inside the society.'[27]

Some Asian voices

Most Asian commentators found something to criticize in the book, though they certainly did not speak in unison. Krishna Prakash Gupta, then a Ph.D. candidate in Social Relations at Harvard, took issue with Myrdal's conception of 'Asian values', which contrasted an 'historically rational West and irrational East.' His interpretation of 'preconditions,' she argued, 'overlooks the current recognition by social scientists that Asian institutional forms are in fact highly adaptable to development. Had Myrdal studied Japan, he would have found that kinship ties, paternalism, and many other "obstacles" are not necessarily inimical to economic development.'[28] Writing in *Yojana* (an organ of India's Ministry of Information and Broadcasting), journalist Ramesh Thapar faulted the book for relying on 'outdated thought' and for failing to take adequate account of 'the agricultural revolution underway in India.' Further, 'the poverty of nations is inquired into without any solid reference to the depradation of the colonial era . . . ' He added, 'Had Myrdal been bolder in his probe, he would have detailed the role of colonialism in building the vital surplus for the industrialization of the West, he would have understood that aid to Asia is seen by Asians as a debt repaid . . . ' Thapar concluded that 'the foreign expert needs to look at the world from Delhi and Peking rather than from London, Washington and Stockholm.'[29]

S. Shukla, Professor of Education at the Jamia Milia Islamic in New Delhi, attacked Myrdal for 'ethnocentrisms' in his approach to educational policy. 'His main trouble,' Shukla wrote, 'is the Asian company he keeps (or quotes!). All of his sources and professional contacts are Western educated or influenced members of the educated *elite* that controls power and culture in Asian societies, particularly India.' These people, the reviewer asserted, were 'more affected by Western modes of educational development than is good for them.' Genuine development would involve 'changes in social structure, that is, in the pattern of relationships, power and wealth, as between social groups, modern or traditional, as between castes and tribes, or as between classes.' Myrdal's basic problem was diagnosed as stemming from a desire 'for the achievement of development within the existing social framework. Myrdal is, therefore, disinclined to be too critical of the Western-educated intelligentsia which leads this system.'[30]

Rohit Dava, writing in a journal published in Bombay, took issue with the tone of pessimism that resounded throughout the book. Changes were underway that brightened the region's prospects. 'It would be incorrect,' he observed, 'to give an impression that planners are oblivious of the human factors involved in translating a policy into programme or that the Asian agriculturalist is so backward that it is difficult to communicate to him the advantages of better farming methods and even in investing in agriculture.'[31] Pessimism was also challenged by S. S. Wagle, who maintained that 'with economic growth, the main springs of the self-reforming national character may again revive. A glimpse of this is seen to some extent in the metropolitan cities of Asia where industrial labour and urban societies have little time to observe religious taboos, superstitious customs of caste norms, and seem to be relatively responsive to rational and progressive thinking.' He accepted Myrdal's characterization of 'soft states,' but insisted that this phenomenon should be interpreted differently: 'During the colonial period a deep-felt antipathy and non-co-operation with the alien authorities was fostered' and 'it caused an erosion of the sense of social obligation.' In addition, he suggested that Myrdal's 'political understanding' was suspect because it 'seems to be closely shadowed by the American (USA) foreign policy, which adopts a paternalistic know-all about the Indian polity.'[32]

Of particular interest was the reaction of P. C. Mahalanobis, the principal architect of India's Second Five-Year Plan, with its emphasis on priority to heavy industry. (This bit of his handiwork had been a target of negative criticism in *Asian Drama*.) He accepted the book's discussion of bureaucratic delays and corruption (though he maintained that the latter was less prevalent in India than in some of the other countries). But he regarded the critique of India's technical planning as 'misconceived.' The Second Five-Year Plan (1955–1956 to 1960–1961) could not be faulted for failure to take long-term considerations into account. He insisted that 'the strategy for the domestic manufacture of machinery to set up factories to produce fertilizers was adopted essentially on the basis of long-term considerations.' India, he argued, 'was no longer stagnant. . . . The industrial growth which has started in India is likely to gain momentum, even if slowly, and help in the modernization of Indian society.' He closed a lengthy review on a respectful note: 'I have expressed my views frankly. This is the only way in which I can pay my homage to a very great man who has written a great book with the highest sense of intellectual integrity and with intense sympathy and anguish for the poverty and stagnation on one-fourth of the world's population who live in the countries of South Asia.'[33]

Asian Drama revisited

Some 15 years after *Asian Drama* was published, Myrdal returned to this topic in a paper prepared at the invitation of the World Bank to appear in a volume honoring the pioneers in development economics. He reiterated his commitment to institutional research that exposed the unreliability and unsuitability of analytic concepts constructed in advanced countries to the realities of the underdeveloped ones. And he held fast to the 'conviction that egalitarian institutional reforms to raise the consumption levels of the poor would be the condition for a more rapid development by increasing the productivity of their people.' But he confessed to 'growing pangs of conscience' arising from his original unqualified support to financial assistance flowing from developed countries to the underdeveloped ones. He remained in favor of continued flows of aid, but called for a rethinking of the way it should be directed. He had arrived at this conclusion because of his increasing disenchantment with the political elites in charge of governments in the region who appeared to be increasingly out-of-touch with the needs of their peoples. In his opinion, aid for 'industrial projects, particularly large-scale ones' should be discontinued. The only development aid he supported 'under present circumstances would be directed to the simplest and least costly measures to increase food production, to provide sanitation facilities and to increase their utilization, generally to supply pure water, and also as far as possible to improve health care, particularly for poor families, and to give their children somewhat more of better schooling.' Further, aid-giving governments should not defer to the recipient ones, but should insist on controlling the use of resources they made available.[34]

In 2002, Paul Streeten and Adeel Malik conducted a further revisitation. In their view, there was still cogency in Myrdal's critique of the 'soft state' – witness the widespread incidence of tax evasion. Corruption – the scholarly discussion of which Myrdal was the first to open up – remained a serious issue, distorting the allocation of resources and slowing potential growth rates. The book's critique of the inappropriateness of conventional Western analytic categories in South Asia remained highly relevant. So also was its insistence that the paramount importance of agriculture should not be overshadowed by policies motivated by a pro-industrial bias. There was plenty left to applaud in a study then a third of a century on.[35]

From the 1960s, there have been many highly visible changes in South Asian countries, particularly in the modern sectors that attract attention in a jet-set culture. In India particularly, the revolution in information technology has created impressively attractive jobs for computer programmers. High technology in communication has also brought a new affluence to cities like Bangalore, where superb, well-trained operators handle the toll-free telephone traffic directed to a fair number of prominent US corporations. Such a development would have been unthinkable in the above-mentioned period. Not only was the needed technology then lacking: Services of this sort were held not to be internationally tradeable.

Though there have been some remarkable transformations, a fundamental truth persists. The bulk of the populations of these countries remain locked in an agricultural system in which labor is far from fully utilized and stricken by poverty. For a time, the Green Revolution brightened their prospects. In the early 1970s, India, for example, had achieved self-sufficiency in food grains. By 2006, that is no longer the case.

A possible parallel?

Myrdal always regarded himself as a child of the Enlightenment. Its glorification of the virtues of rationality was a lodestone of his intellectual career. There is a possible parallel between his intellectual style and that of one of the key figures among the philosophical radicals who contributed to the shaping of the Enlightenment in the first instance. James Mill (1773–1836) also embraced the Enlightenment faith in the powers of reason. Nowadays he is perhaps best remembered as the father of John Stuart Mill. This does him less than justice. In his own time, he had close working relationship with both David Ricardo and Jeremy Bentham. He wrote a well-regarded book in the genre of classical political economy, in which a statement of a 'law of markets' (subsequently identified as Say's Law) first appeared.

In addition, he wrote about India and later became involved in the administration of East India affairs.

Mill's *History of British India* appeared in three volumes in 1817. It took him a decade to complete – a much longer period than he had anticipated when he embarked on the project. (It should be noted that British India, as configured at that time, included the present-day Pakistan and Bangladesh, along with India proper.) Mill never set foot on the subcontinent, but he certainly did not regard that as a disqualification for this undertaking. The essential qualification for the task, as he saw it, was 'a most profound knowledge of the laws of human nature' and 'of the principles of human society.'[36]

What is of interest here is the way this Enlightenment figure interpreted Indian society. He was especially harsh about what he perceived to be the 'rude' and decadent state of Hindu society. (He was much more sympathetic to Muslim society, which had, after all, made important contributions to that most rational of all disciplines – mathematics.) But Hindu society and institutions were built around an 'uncontrollable sway of superstition.'[37] He was devastating in his indictment of the caste system, describing it as 'that institution which stands a more effectual barrier against the good of human nature than any other institution which the workings of caprice and of selfishness have ever produced.' He added, 'The most irrational practice that ever found existence in the agriculture of any nation is general in India . . . ' He even put a negative spin on the skill of the Hindu in weaving (which was widely admired in Europe). For Mill, it was not remarkable that the Hindu should find weaving congenial. This craft, he observed, was a sedentary occupation and 'thus in harmony with his predominant inclination.' Moreover, it called for little bodily exertion, 'of which he is always exceedingly sparing, and the finer the production, the more slender the force which he is called upon to supply.'[38]

Though obviously much has changed to differentiate the British India that Mill wrote about in the early nineteenth century from the subcontinent that was the focus of *Asian Drama*, there are some lingering continuities in a style of Enlightenment thinking. After completing his massive study, Mill joined the staff of the East India Company and became in effect the economic policy planner for British India. (His son, John Stuart Mill, was to succeed him in that position.) Myrdal would take sharp issue with the way the Mills performed in that assignment. They proposed to use the Ricardian theory of differential rent as the basis for a land tax in British India and managed to have it implemented in part of the subcontinent. This was a misappropriation of the latest innovation in Western economic theorizing of the kind that *Asian Drama* denounced.

In addition, there was a fundamental disjunction separating Myrdal's insistence on the promotion of democratic values from the careers of both Mills, who were parties to the practice of despotic paternalism.

Notes

1. G. Myrdal to N. S. Buchanan, The Rockefeller Foundation, 19 June 1956, as quoted by J. Angresano, *The Political Economy of Gunnar Myrdal* (Cheltenham, UK: Edward Elgar, 1997), p. 78.
2. Ibid., p. 79.
3. G. Myrdal to A. Heckscher, 18 September 1961, as quoted by J. Angresano, op. cit., p. 79.
4. Altogether, six were listed as 'Principal Assistants' in the three volumes published in 1968. Two were from Britain (P. P. Streeten, then at the University of Sussex, and D. Wightman of the University of Birmingham); two from the United States (W. J. Barber of Wesleyan University and G. W. Wilson of the University of Indiana); one from Finland (A. Majava, Demographer at the National Planning Office); and A. Myrdal, then a member of the Swedish Cabinet. In addition, K. Azfar and M. Lipton, recent graduates of Balliol College, Oxford, served as research assistants, circa 1960–1961.
5. G. Myrdal, *Asian Drama*, Vol. 1, pp. 57–67. Italics in the original.
6. As quoted by S. Bok, *Alva Myrdal: A Daughter's Memoir* (Reading, MA: Addison Wesley Publishing company, 1991), p. 289.
7. G. Myrdal to A. Heckscher, 1 October 1966, as quoted by J. Angresano, op. cit., p. 79.
8. G. Myrdal, *Asian Drama*, Vol. 1, p. xi.
9. Ibid., p. xii.
10. Ibid.
11. Ibid., p. 19.
12. A full statement of the relevant arguments can be found in *Asian Drama*, Appendix 6, 'A Critical Appraisal of the Concept and Theory of Underemployment.'
13. The definitive statement of the issues involved here is to be found in *Asian Drama*, Appendix 3, 'Economic Models and Their Usefulness for Planning in South Asia,' written by P. Streeten.
14. G. Myrdal, *Asian Drama* Prologue, pp. 30–31.
15. *Asian Drama*, p. 1188.

16. Ibid., p. 1239.
17. Ibid., p. 1378.
18. Ibid., pp. 1378, 1380.
19. T. Balogh, 'The Scrutable East,' *New York Times Book Review* (24 March 1968) 1.
20. K. E. Boulding, 'Asia: Soft States and Hard Facts,' *New Republic*, 157 (4 May 1968) 25–8.
21. G. Rosen, Review of 'Asian Drama,' *American Economic Review*, LVIII:5:Pt 1 (December 1968) 1397–1401.
22. H. Myint, Review of 'Asian Drama,' *Swedish Journal of Economics*, 70 (1968) 242–45.
23. J. Fischer, 'Western Intellectuals vs. Myrdal's Brutal Facts,' *Harper's Magazine* (June 1968) 12, 16, 18–19.
24. P. T. Bauer, 'Million-word Pamphlet,' *Spectator*, 222 (10 January 1969) 44–45.
25. G. F. Papanek, Review of 'Asian Drama,' *The American Journal of Sociology*, 74 (July 1968) 308–10.
26. *Times Literary Supplement* (21 November 1968) 12979–99.
27. C. Geertz, 'Myrdal's Mythology: "Modernism" and the Third World,' *Encounter*, XXXIII:1 (July 1969) 26–34.
28. K. P. Gupta, Review of 'Asian Drama,' *Commonwealth*, LXXXIX:1 (4 October 1968) 35–36.
29. R. Thapar, 'Poverty of Nations or Notions,' *Yojana* (12 May 1968) 2–6.
30. S. Shukla, 'Planning and Educational Development,' *Indian Educational Review*, 5 (July 1970) 156–65.
31. R. Dave, *Commerce* (29 July 1968) 146–47.
32. S. S. Wagle, 'An Inquiry Into the Poverty of Nations,' *United Asia*, 20 (August 1968) 202–09.
33. P. C. Mahalanobis, 'The Asian Drama: an Indian View,' *Economic and Political Weekly* (Bombay, July 1969) 1119–32.
34. G. Myrdal, 'International Inequality and Foreign Aid in Retrospect,' *Pioneers in Development*, G. M. Meier and D. Seers, eds (New York: Oxford University Press, published for the World Bank, 1984), pp. 151–65.
35. P. Streeten and A. Malik, 'Asian Drama Revisited,' *The South Asian Challenge*, K. Haq, ed. (Bangalore: Oxford University Press, 2002), pp. 33–71.
36. J. Mill, *The History of British India* (London: Baldwin, Cradock, and Joy, 1817), Vol. 1, p. xix.
37. Ibid., p. 131.
38. Ibid., pp. 628, 348, 342. For a fuller discussion of Mill's thinking, see W. J. Barber, *British Economic Thought and India, 1600–1858* (Oxford: Clarendon Press, 1975), especially Chapters 8 and 10.

10
Economic Policy Advice-Giving for the Rich and the Poor in the 1960s and 1970s

In the later stages of his prolific career, Myrdal published two volumes that recorded his mature thinking about economic policy-making. Both built on analytic foundations laid in his previous works. Both had their origins in invited lectures in the United States. Both had the noun 'challenge' in their titles.

The context of *Challenge to Affluence* (1963)

This work – which spoke to the condition of the American economy – reconnected Myrdal with some of his thinking of the 1930s about the determinants of national income and output. It will be recalled that his *Monetary Equilibrium*, originally published in 1932, and his memoranda for the Swedish government soon thereafter anticipated central insights concerning macro-economic theory and policy that were to be associated in the English-speaking world with the Keynesian revolution.

Myrdal returned to these themes in the early 1960s, at a time of widespread dissatisfaction with the performance of the US economy. The economic growth rate was then sluggish and, in the eyes of some, there was a risk that the Soviet economy might outpace the United States. Meanwhile, the country was experiencing persistent unemployment at a rate of roughly six and one-half percent of the labor force. President John F. Kennedy had pledged in the campaign of 1960 to 'get the country moving again.' Once in office, fulfillment of that pledge proved to be more difficult than had been anticipated.

Kennedy had appointed a strong team to the Council of Economic Advisers (CEA). It was composed of three academic economists, all Keynesians: Walter Heller, Chairman (University of Minnesota), James Tobin (Yale), and Kermit Gordon (Williams College). They were united in the conviction that an increase in aggregate demand would eliminate unemployment, other than the transitional variety: a measured four percent rate of unemployment was thus regarded as 'full employment.' Government measures to augment aggregate demand could also stimulate the rate of economic growth. A fiscal stimulant could, of course, be accomplished by reducing taxes, increasing government spending, or by some combination of the two. The CEA's Keynesians were persuaded that tax-cutting was the route to be preferred. Timing here was a crucial consideration: a tax cut would increase the public's spending power immediately (and a stimulant to the economy could be expected soon thereafter), whereas a program of increased public spending would necessarily be delayed by debates over allocations and project design, by solicitations for competitive bidding, and so on. The 1962 *Economic Report of the President* (written by the CEA) mapped out this strategy in detail and was regarded as a textbook in applied Keynesian economics.

Within official Washington, there was formidable resistance to this design for economic policy. Congressional opinion was heavily influenced by the doctrine that the course of wisdom required the Federal government to balance its budgets annually. This view had supplied the keystone of economic policy in the preceding Eisenhower administration. (The attempt to apply this principle had triggered a sharp recession in 1957–1958; the downturn in the national income reduced tax receipts and thus generated the largest peacetime deficit in the Federal accounts that had been recorded to that date. The doctrinaires on the primacy of balanced budgets were disposed to overlook that inconvenient fact.)

But there were also nodes of resistance to deliberate deficits – achieved by tax-cutting – elsewhere in official Washington. The Treasury Department, charged with the management of the country's gold reserves, was concerned that accelerated economic expansion might worsen a gold hemorrhage that was already visible. The management of the country's central bank – the Federal Reserve Board of Governors, led by Chairman William McChesney Martin – was unpersuaded by the CEA analysis for another reason. In its view, the observed rate of unemployment, though unfortunate, could not be cured by fiscal stimulants. This phenomenon was 'structural,' not cyclical, and reflected the fact that those who lost jobs in the declining sectors of the economy lacked the skill qualifications needed to find work in the expanding ones. Within this analytic framework, fiscal measures to increase aggregate demand would not provide work for the workless, but would touch off dangerous inflationary pressures. There was yet another dissident voice within Kennedy's official family. Kennedy had appointed John Kenneth Galbraith, a Harvard economist and personal friend, to be the Ambassador to India. Galbraith had recently published a book entitled *The Affluent Society*, in which he juxtaposed the wealth of the country's private sector and the poverty of the public sector. In his reading of matters, top priority should be assigned to increased spending to improve education and health care and to remove urban blight. A tax cut that would reward those who were already well off would be a mistake.[1]

Myrdal's contribution to the American discourse

Myrdal opened *Challenge to Affluence* by asserting that the United States 'has lagged in applying the new knowledge we have about how to induce economic progress, and the new determination we have acquired to use this knowledge to our advantage. And as we shall show in this book, this unfortunate backwardness in American economic policy has serious effects not only for the welfare of large sections of its own people but also for the direction and effectiveness of its foreign policy.'[2] He was certainly well aware of the Keynesian orientation of Kennedy's CEA and of the analytic thinking that underpinned its recommendations on economic policy. Yet he criticized economists who 'continue[d] to reason in an unrealistic Keynesian way.'[3]

The basis for this criticism can be traced to Myrdal's findings when he wrote *An American Dilemma*. He had then come directly to grips with the handicaps Negroes experienced in their attempts to compete for attractive jobs in the labor market. Though barriers of discrimination had begun to come down by 1962–1963, the competitive position of Negroes was still compromised by inadequacies in skills and training. America, he feared, faced the prospect of living with a permanent 'underclass' of unemployed and unemployables. In language reminiscent of *An American Dilemma*, he described this situation as incompatible with the 'American creed' and appealed to the nation's conscience to address it. In his view, it should be recognized that 'rapid and steady growth and full employment' were not possible 'without taking vigorous measures within the American nation to induce greater equality of opportunity and of standards of living.'[4] It should be noted here that Myrdal's conception of 'full employment' was different from the one current in official Washington. He found it 'discouraging' that the 'Kennedy administration has redefined tolerable unemployment to be as high as 4 per cent.'[5] This failed to take into account the part-time unemployed and the underemployment of those functioning at low productivity levels.

In Myrdal's judgment, Americans should set their policy goals much more ambitiously. A thoroughgoing attack on unemployment and underemployment should begin by recognizing the 'structural' dimension of the problem. (This adjective made Kennedy's CEA skittish – it sounded too much like the Federal Reserve's resistance to fiscal stimulation.) What Myrdal meant by the term was a 'discrepancy... between the type of labor supplied and demanded.'[6] It could be corrected only through a vigorous program of education and training for those on the fringe of the labor force. Prospects for success in that effort would be enhanced if fiscal policies produced an environment of expansion, but Keynesian-style fiscal strategies would fail to do the job on their own. Indeed, he described 'conventional economic analysis' of the Keynesian variety as 'superficial.'[7]

In addition to the book, Myrdal found other outlets for his message: an article in early 1963 in the *New Republic* – entitled 'Getting America Moving' – borrowed from the Kennedy administration's vocabulary. His recommendations for action, however, went well beyond what the Executive Branch then had in mind. He supported tax cuts 'to give a spurt to the economy,' but held that major increases in government spending, especially for education and training, were also essential. He feared that changes in the structure of the American labor force had tended to 'increase the class chasms in American society and to stiffen the class structure.' This was happening because 'technological progress does not release labor in a uniform way but directs labor demand more and more toward the highly skilled and highly educated. The incidence of unemployment tends increasingly to fall most heavily upon those who for social and economic reasons have lesser skill and lesser education.'[8] In addition, he pushed his position in an interview with *Business Week* and at a luncheon meeting of the Senate Sub-committee on Employment and Manpower in December 1963.[9]

The Challenge of World Poverty: A World Anti-Poverty Program in Outline (1970)

In the Preface to this study, Myrdal informed his readers that he had originally intended to close *Asian Drama* with a discussion of the policy implications of his findings. But, given the 'unwieldy length' of that three-volume study, a 'comprehensive epitome of main policies the underdeveloped and developed countries should follow' was not included. The 1970 volume could thus be understood as an effort to 'fill this void' – or, put slightly differently, it could be regarded as the 'missing eighth part' of *Asian Drama*.[10] A qualification was in order here. The later study could not be an exact statement of what might have appeared in the earlier one. After all, there was an announced difference in scope: The 1970 document was addressed to the world, not just to South Asia. Though attention to this distinction is worth noting, it was nevertheless the case that the overwhelming bulk of the documentation and supporting footnotes was drawn from *Asian Drama*.

Myrdal acknowledged an additional motivation prompting him to write *The Challenge of World Poverty*. He had been dismayed that *Asian Drama* had often been 'mistaken as rendering arguments for not bothering to try to aid the underdeveloped countries in their development efforts, which pleased the conservatives and still more the reactionaries in Western countries.' Some of his liberal friends were also 'under the same false impression.'[11] The new work afforded an opportunity to set matters straight. It was structured to distinguish the lines of policy recommended for the underdeveloped countries, on the one hand, from the policies that he believed the developed countries should pursue.

Discussion of issues of primary importance to the underdeveloped world was positioned within the framework developed in *Asian Drama*: that is, a recognition that the central problem arose from the fact that growth in population (and in the potential labor force) was such that the feasible expansions in an industrial base could not provide productive employment for this increment in the decades immediately ahead. This meant that focus on the agricultural sector deserved a high priority for policy-makers. The objective of their interventions should be to encourage labor-intensive innovations that would enable farm outputs to grow, while the agricultural sector simultaneously absorbed more workers. If this were to be made to happen, a coordinated package of measures would be needed. It would be insufficient to treat individual innovations in isolation. The availability of improved irrigation facilities, for example, might offer the potential for multiple cropping that would both raise outputs and absorb additional labor. But such a favorable outcome could not be taken for granted. A successful result called for a wider program that would include, among other things, extension work to educate farmers on ways to take advantage of new techniques, improved access to credit to finance fertilizers and higher-yielding varieties of seeds, expanded marketing and storage facilities, and so on. But along with all this, Myrdal maintained that 'the people, bound up in agriculture, must acquire an ambition that today is often missing if they are to raise their incomes and levels of living. Inducing them to do that, and getting them to raise their technology from a primitive level, requires an educational effort of staggering dimensions.'[12]

But creating an environment in which such change could be accomplished faced a major impediment in most poor countries, namely the 'inegalitarian social and economic stratification that prevailed in most poor countries.' As Myrdal put it, '*What is broadly referred to as the problem of "land reform" or "agrarian reform," tenancy reform included, has to be attacked in order to create a situation where the labor force has the opportunities, and feels the incentives, to exert itself very much more.*'[13] He regarded the widespread system of sharecropping as particularly reprehensible, arguing that it was 'conducive neither to technological change nor to investments in labor and money, nor, generally, to . . . increases in quantity and quality of labor input. . . . The sharecropper, often paying the landowner more than half of the gross yield of the land he tills, is held down in poverty and apathy.'[14]

These arguments, of course, were familiar from *Asian Drama*. But the case made here for a more egalitarian economic structure as indispensable to a successful agricultural strategy over the longer term was stated, perhaps, with even greater passion. Similarly, there would appear to be a heightened sense of disappointment about failures of leadership to promote meaningful land reform. There was lots of talk, but little action.

Given this situation, he concluded – as he had in *Asian Drama* – that rewarding capitalist farmers (who responded to economic incentives) and penalizing idle landowners (through targeted tax policies) was probably the best, though suboptimal, approach.

In *The Challenge of World Poverty*, Myrdal examined one topic that had not figured in *Asian Drama*. The 'Green Revolution' – with the introduction of high-yielding varieties of seeds on a substantial scale – had occurred too late to be commented on in the earlier study. This development had been hailed as a breakthrough that would transform agriculture in the underdeveloped world. He was critical of 'this outburst of technocratic optimism' on grounds that it had been 'used to undergird the flight from the need of large-scale reforms of one type or another of land ownership and tenure...' In his view, the full promise of the 'Green Revolution' could not be realized otherwise. In its absence, 'the availability of the new seed grains will join the other forces of reaction that are now tending to increase inequality among the rural populations in underdeveloped countries.'[15]

Myrdal further addressed this issue in a paper presented to the International Association of Agricultural Economists, meeting in Minsk, USSR, in the late summer of 1970. He there attacked the 'technocratic euphoria' spawned by the 'Green Revolution' that had effectively buried further consideration of land reforms. He then wrote, '... the new opportunities are open only to farmers with irrigated land and with capital resources to buy fertilizers and other necessities and implements for intensive farming.... To the larger part of the subsistence cultivators, whether working as share-croppers or on mini-farms of their own, the new opportunities are out of reach.'[16]

Myrdal's policy agenda for the poor countries gave agriculture pride of place, but it did not stop there. He urged their governments to take family planning seriously and to build an administrative apparatus fitted for that purpose that could deploy a strong staff of medical and paramedical personnel. In addition, he called for fundamental reform in the educational systems. In substantial degree, the existing educational structure was 'too academic' and produced too many generalists. All of this tended to perpetuate a bias against manual work. Teaching – at all levels – should be reoriented in the direction of technical and vocational training. Access to education should also be opened to all segments of society. Unfortunately, the power structure in these countries usually resisted such reforms, and this, in turn, exacerbated inequalities.[17]

In *Asian Drama*, Myrdal had been vigorous in his critique of 'soft states' and of the corruption associated with that condition. His reform agenda called for the strengthening of central administrations. This might well mean 'retrenchment' in their size: there was typically too much personnel-padding in their bureaucracies, and their officialdom contained too many with questionable competence. As a partial buffer to corruption, he recommended that administrative discretion in the implementation of policies be minimized in favor of regulations that could be applied uniformly across the board. Bureaucratic discretion in the award of licenses, permits, and contracts invited bribes from those interested in buying preferential treatment. A leaner bureaucracy of the competent should be rewarded with higher salaries. This would diminish temptation to accept bribes.[18]

In *The Challenge to World Poverty*, Myrdal did not address exhaustively all of the policies he had discussed in *Asian Drama*. Treatment of industrialization programs is a case in point. In the earlier work, he had spoken favorably of an industrial strategy guided by a policy of import substitution. In the later work, this matter was touched upon briefly and much less approvingly. In this connection, he noted that 'the import restrictions which most underdeveloped economies have been forced to adopt are made necessary by their foreign-exchange difficulties.' These expedients also provided a measure of protection for producers engaged in import substitution. It was thus 'possible for high-cost producers to do a profitable business at home.' But this situation was not altogether healthy. 'By insulating the internal market from foreign competition, it blunts incentives to produce commodities for export.'[19]

The bulk of the policies recommended above, Myrdal argued, '*must be carried out by the underdeveloped countries themselves.*'[20] There were a few exceptions. The developed world could make a significant contribution by providing funding and expertise for agricultural research in tropical environments. And foreigners might help to improve the probity of public administration in developing countries if they disciplined the behavior of their own nationals. In Myrdal's judgment, 'it is self-evident that an *abstention by Western business firms from bribing their way into the economic life of underdeveloped countries would be a very substantial aid to those countries in their attempts to overcome the disabilities of being soft states*...'[21]

In addition, economists from the developed world could, in principle, make an important contribution if their researches in the underdeveloped countries provided an improved understanding of their realities. This would have 'a wholesome influence' on the formulation of policies. Unfortunately, all too few of those engaged in this activity rose to its challenges. As Myrdal diagnosed matters, 'the main bias of research on underdeveloped countries at present... is that we abstract from attitudes, institutions, and the productivity effects of levels of living when those are very low.' He added, 'A more unbiased and penetrating research effort' promised to '*give more impetus to the progressive forces that raise demand for radical reform.*'[22]

The type of research needed would have to begin with 'critical scrutiny' of the available statistical material. Too often this failed to happen in the rush to build 'impressive-looking econometric models.' This critique of professional practice echoed themes discussed at length in *Asian Drama*. But his choice of language this time around carried with it a sharper bite: 'It is difficult to avoid the conclusion that *the last generation of economists, with all talk about rigor and precision, have lowered scientific standards in precisely these respects.*'[23]

Stipulating the responsibilities of the developed countries

When reviewing the role the developed countries should play in relieving the plight of the underdeveloped ones, Myrdal reiterated a number of points he had set out earlier in *An International Economy* in 1958. He maintained – contrary to the arguments of standard international trade theory – that the international trading system, as it had evolved, had been a mechanism that promoted greater international inequalities. In large measure, this situation could best be understood in terms of the relative weights of 'backwash' and 'spread effects' in poor countries. In their circumstances, openness to international commerce meant that the 'backwash effects' – the negative impacts on domestic employment and income arising from foreign competition – had been strong. Meanwhile, the 'spread effects' – that is, the capacity of increased export earnings to stimulate expanded domestic economic activity – had been weak. Redressing the imbalances in the international economy, as he saw it, was a moral issue. He invited his readers to engage with a 'conception of *a welfare world*' in which a 'created harmony' at the international level was brought into being.[24]

He recognized, of course, that the reality of the international scene was a long distance removed from that ideal. Indeed, it was further removed by 1970 than it had been in 1958. He held the United States responsible for the bulk of this backsliding. Its foreign aid budgets had been shrunk over the decade-plus years in question with a shift of resources to the conduct of military operations in Vietnam. (Myrdal was vehemently opposed to this action – which he described as cruel, criminal, immoral, and illegal – and he served as chairman of an international committee investigating US War Crimes in Vietnam.) The manner in which the diminished sums had been allocated was also objectionable. Decisions about beneficiaries – and about the sums they were to receive – had been guided by political considerations, not humanitarian ones. The prevalence of 'tied loans' – that is, export credits that obliged beneficiaries to buy from the donor country – further disadvantaged aid recipients.

Even though the exercise was visionary, Myrdal sketched out a picture of what a healthier international economic order might look like. At a minimum, developed countries should reserve a substantial part of their expected increases in national income for transfer to the poor ones. (Ultimately, he hoped that a progressive system of international taxation could be put in place that would move the distribution of world incomes in an egalitarian direction.) In the ideal situation, resources thus made available should be distributed by a multilateral inter-governmental authority. In the near term, developed countries should at least move quickly to open their markets to exports from the underdeveloped world by removing discriminations against these products.[25] There was a radical quality as well in Myrdal's recommendations on the uses to which aid funds should be put. He was well aware of an argument advanced by opponents of foreign aid appropriations to the effect that funds would not be used for genuine developmental purposes, but would instead line the pockets of those at the top of inegalitarian power structures. It made sense to blunt that argument by insisting that foreign aid should assign a priority to supporting reforms – such as the land reforms that

Myrdal favored – to benefit the masses. But this strategy, he insisted, was the right one to pursue on its own merits. He wrote that he was firmly convinced that *'only by appealing to peoples' moral feelings will it be possible to create the popular basis for increasing aid to underdeveloped countries as substantially as is needed.'*[26] When people were fully informed and their moral feelings aroused, 'they will demand that aid not be used to pamper the oligarchies. They will demand that aid be given to countries making serious efforts toward social reform and indeed that it be given on condition that such reforms are undertaken; indeed the aid may be given to make such reforms possible.'[27]

Myrdal was later to modify his position on this matter. As was noted in the preceding chapter, he confessed in 1984 to 'growing pangs of conscience' when recalling his earlier enthusiasm for foreign aid for the underdeveloped world. This disillusionment stemmed from his judgment that the promise of foreign aid to benefit the poor had not been realized. Instead it had propped up corrupt regimes.

Notes

1. For details on the infighting over macro-economic policy in the early 1960s, see W. J. Barber, 'The Kennedy Years: Purposeful Pedagogy,' *Exhortation and Controls: The Search for a Wage-Price Policy, 1945–1971*, C. D. Goodwin, ed. (Washington, DC: The Brookings Institution, 1975), pp. 135–91.
2. G. Myrdal, *Challenge to Affluence* (New York: Pantheon Books, 1963), p. 4.
3. Ibid., p. 30.
4. Ibid., p. 7.
5. Ibid., p. 40.
6. Ibid., p. 24.
7. Ibid., p. 23.
8. G. Myrdal, 'Getting America Moving,' *New Republic*, 148 (26 January 1963) 15–20.
9. 'Good Friend and Critic,' *Business Week* (14 December 1963) 57–60.
10. G. Myrdal, *The Challenge of World Poverty: a World Anti-poverty Program in Outline* (New York: Pantheon Books, 1970), pp. ix, 251.
11. Ibid., pp. ix–x.
12. Ibid., p. 58.
13. Ibid., p. 100; italics in the original.
14. Ibid., p. 100.
15. Ibid., pp. 124–25.

16. G. Myrdal, paper presented to the International Association of Agricultural Economists, Minsk, USSR, as published under the title 'Are the Developing Countries Really Developing?', *Bulletin of the Atomic Scientists*, 27 (January 1971) 5–8.
17. *The Challenge of World Poverty*, pp. 194–207, passim.
18. Ibid., pp. 243–51, *passim*.
19. Ibid., p. 287.
20. Ibid., p. 254; italics in the original.
21. Ibid., p. 252; italics in the original.
22. Ibid., p. 258; italics in the original.
23. Ibid., p. 269; italics in the original.
24. Ibid., p. 298; italics in the original.
25. Ibid., p. 364 ff.
26. Ibid., p. 368; italics in the original.
27. Ibid., p. 372.

Epilogue

In October 1974, the Royal Swedish Academy of Sciences announced that it had named Gunnar Myrdal and Friedrich von Hayek as co-winners of the Nobel Memorial Prize in Economics. The citation accompanying this announcement merits quotation at length.

> Since the Economics Prize was inaugurated, the names of two economists, whose research has reached beyond pure economic science, have always been on the list of proposed prizewinners: Gunnar Myrdal and Friedrich von Hayek. They both began their research careers with significant works in the field of pure *economic* theory. In the main their early work – in the twenties and thirties – was in the same fields: theory of economic fluctuations and monetary theory. Since then both economists have widened their horizons to include broad aspects of social and institutional phenomena.
>
> Mainly by directing most of his research to economic problems in the broadest sense, particularly the negro problem in the United States and poverty in the developing countries, Myrdal has sought to relate economic analysis to social, demographic, and institutional conditions. Von Hayek has extended his field of study to embrace such elements as the legal framework of economic systems and issues concerning the way individuals, organizations, and various social systems function. Both have been deeply interested in problems of economic policy and have therefore also studied changes in the organizational, institutional, and legal conditions in our societies.
>
> A quality which Myrdal and von Hayek have in common is a well-documented ability to find new and original ways of posing questions and presenting new ideas on causes and policies. This characteristic has often made them somewhat controversial. This is only natural when the field of research is extended to include factors and linkages which economists usually take for granted or neglect.

With respect to Myrdal's distinctive contributions, the selection committee directed attention to *The Political Element in the Development of Economic Theory*, describing it as 'a pioneering critique of how political values in many areas of research are inserted into economic analysis.' It further noted that the Academy of Sciences had 'attached great importance to the monumental work *An American Dilemma . . . ,*' observing that Myrdal had there 'documented his ability to combine economic analysis with a broad sociological perspective.' The citation added that 'Myrdal's extensive research into the problems of the developing countries is very much of the same nature as *An American Dilemma*. This, too, is economic and sociological research in the broadest sense, where great significance is attached to political, institutional, demographic, educational and health factors.'[1]

The Royal Academy's announcement displayed some artful draftsmanship. The emphasis on parallelisms in the careers of the co-winners amounted to an attempt to defuse some potential tensions. In that regard, the exercise was not altogether successful.

Myrdal's reaction to the award

Myrdal was in New York City when a telephone message from Stockholm informed him of the award. He later remarked to a reporter: 'If I had not been a bit asleep when they called me early in the morning in the U.S., I would have said no.'[2] Indeed he was later to argue that the Economics Prize itself should be abolished. These, however, were latter-day views. In the 1960s, he had been very active in soliciting funds from banker friends in Stockholm to endow a Nobel Memorial Prize in Economics. The thought that he might have a personal stake in this was rather ill disguised. In 1972, he was certainly not disposed to turn down this award. His disaffection with the Nobel Memorial Prize in Economics came later when he perceived it to be subject to bias and manipulation.

Even so, he was not totally at ease with the selectors' decisions in 1974. The sticking point here was being paired with von Hayek for the award. Throughout their careers, they had worked from opposite ends of the ideological spectrum. Von Hayek had consistently been an uncompromising champion of *laissez-faire* who regarded government interventions as the source of problems. Myrdal, by contrast, clearly doubted that uninhibited markets could be counted on to get things right and, when they failed, government action should be called upon to provide a corrective. On at least two occasions, there was some personal friction between them. In 1933, von Hayek published a version in German of Myrdal's analysis of monetary equilibrium in a volume he was editing, though he did so reluctantly. He made no bones about the fact that he fundamentally disagreed with its argument. Not long thereafter, von Hayek – then at the London School of Economics – is believed to have overridden an invitation to Myrdal to deliver a lecture there. For his part, Myrdal distanced himself unambiguously from the arguments that von Hayek had set out in *The Road to Serfdom*. There could be no mistaking his target when Myrdal wrote in 1951 that 'All this popular talk about economic planning leading us straight to the Police State, and so on, is, if you permit me to be blunt, just bunk.'[3]

One of Myrdal's daughters, Sissela Bok, has captured the family mood when the names of the co-winners were announced.

> Sharing the prize in this way was probably as much of a cold shower for von Hayek as it was for Gunnar. The two were polar opposites from a political point of view. Neither they nor anyone else could avoid thinking that the prize was the result of an ideological balancing act. Many among their colleagues even surmised that the choice reflected a condescending joke on the part of members of the Swedish economics establishment. Although they could hardly avoid giving their brilliant but cosmopolitan and flamboyantly un-Swedish compatriot a prize, they had it within their power to do so in a way that prevented him from relishing the honor or feeling truly recognized in his home country.[4]

Alva Myrdal was awarded the Nobel Peace Prize in 1982 in recognition of her work as the Swedish delegate to the Geneva Disarmament Committee. (This marked the only instance in which husband and wife had become Nobel Laureates in different fields.)

The Nobel Memorial Prize acceptance speech

Myrdal swallowed whatever reservations he had when preparing a speech accepting the shared Nobel Memorial Prize. He chose as his title 'The Equality Issue in World Development.' In many respects, his treatment of this topic echoed themes he had set out in *The Challenge of World Poverty*. He sharply criticized the developed world (and particularly the United States) for failure to provide aid that would rise to this challenge. He traced this shortcoming to attempts to mobilize the public in the rich countries with appeals to 'selfish national interests' as the rationale for assisting the poor ones. This tactic, he maintained, did 'not appeal to ordinary people, who in our type of countries determine the course of public policy over the years, while a motivation in moral terms carries weight.'[5] He added that 'when politicians and experts become timid about giving due importance to moral commitments, realism is absent.'[6]

Not only did he castigate the developed countries for their indifference to the needs of the poor, he called upon them to curtail their own consumption. He was in 'deep sympathy,' he reported, 'with the urgings of medical men, environmentalists and other colleagues in the natural sciences, when they speak for the rationality in our own interest, individually and still more collectively, for a much more frugal life style so far as growth in consumption, and production for home consumption, of many material products is concerned.'[7] This would, in turn, free up resources for transfer to the poor. (It will be recalled, however, that Myrdal's enthusiasm for foreign aid was considerably dampened a decade later.) He also returned to a familiar theme when speaking to what the underdeveloped countries needed to do. He called for 'fundamental changes in the conditions under which they are living and working. The important thing is that these changes regularly imply both greater equality and increased productivity at the same time.... To these imperatively needed radical changes belong, first, land reform, but also a fundamental redirection of education and health work. And the "soft state" must be made efficient, and corruption, which is now almost everywhere increasing, must be exterminated on all levels.'[8]

Changes and continuities

The citation prepared by the Nobel Memorial Prize selectors emphasized the shifts in the focus and priorities of Myrdal's intellectual activity over the course of his professional lifetime. He did indeed begin as a pure economic theorist who could practice analytic formalism and speak disdainfully of those who adopted an institutional approach to the discipline. His later work led him to question the claims of mainstream economic theorists to a value-free neutrality in their professional product. He was soon to undertake 'hands-on' engagement in policy-making as a consultant to the Swedish government and as an elected public official. An observer inclined to project a straight-line intellectual trajectory from his beginnings as a pure economic theorist would certainly not have been prepared for the Myrdal who emerged as the author of *An American Dilemma*. This project obviously stretched him in a multidisciplinary direction. And it inspired a conviction that was to remain with him for the remainder of his days that social scientists were in error when attempting to categorize problems as 'economic,' 'political,' 'sociological,' 'historical,' and so on. Such hyphenation was a mistake. There were simply problems, without the qualifiers, and they needed to be embraced in their multidimensional complexity. The Nobel selectors were right when noting that the fundamental approach in *Asian Drama* was an extension of the one adopted in *An American Dilemma*. This was Myrdal reincarnated as an institutional economist and proudly so.

Shifts in the direction of his intellectual odyssey over time are rightly worthy of comment as manifestations of his versatility, originality, and creativity. But this should not obscure that there were continuities as well. From the 1930s onward, he was preoccupied – whatever the specific topic that engaged him – with the question of value judgments in economic and social theorizing. And he was always alert to pillory bogus claims to objectivity and value neutrality. Moreover, in all his work, he deployed a conception he had absorbed from Wicksell – namely the principle of 'cumulative causation,' whether the circle be 'virtuous' or 'vicious.' In addition, he insisted that ideas and ideals had their own autonomy, as well as the capacity to move the flow of events. It is fitting that Myrdal should have the last word. In an address delivered to the annual meeting of the Lutheran Council of the United States in late 1977, he observed that if he were speaking to an audience of social scientists, he 'would stress the need to give human valuations their proper role in research. When social scientists, in their efforts to remain simply "objective," forget that people have a conscience to which they plead, they are in my opinion unrealistic and are not doing their duty as scientists.'[9]

Notes

1. 'The Nobel Memorial Prize in Economics 1974: The Official Announcement of the Royal Academy of Sciences,' as published in the *Swedish Journal of Economics*, 76:4 (December 1974) 469–70. Members of the Economic Science Committee of the Royal Academy of Sciences were as follows: Bertil Ohlin (Chairman), Sune Carlson, Assar Lindbeck, Erik Lundberg, and Herman Wold.
2. As quoted by Richard Swedberg, 'Introduction to the Transaction Edition,' *The Political Element in the Development of Economic Theory* (New Brunswick, NJ: Transaction Publishers, 1990), p. vii.
3. G. Myrdal, 'The Trend Towards Economic Planning,' *The Manchester School of Economic and Social Studies*, XIX:1 (January 1951) 40.
4. S. Bok, *Alva Myrdal: A Daughter's Memoir* (Reading, MA: Addison-Wesley Publishing Co., 1991), p. 305.
5. G. Myrdal, 'The Equality Issue in World Development' (the Nobel Memorial Lecture delivered on 17 March 1975), as published in the *Swedish Journal of Economics*, 77:4 (December 1975) 419. Myrdal was again paired with von Hayek. The latter's Nobel Memorial Lecture was published back-to-back with the former's in the *Swedish Journal of Economics*.
6. Ibid., p. 420.
7. Ibid., p. 424.
8. Ibid., p. 429.
9. G. Myrdal, 'A Worried America,' an address delivered at the tenth annual meeting of the Lutheran Council in the United States, which originally appeared in *Christian Century*, 14 December 1977, as reprinted in *Current*, 202 (April 1978) 57.

Bibliography

Works of Gunnar Myrdal

Books and Monographs (arranged in the order of treatment in the text)

Myrdal, G., *Prisbildningsproblemet och föränderligheten* (The Problem of Price Formation and Changeability), (Uppsala and Stockholm: Almquist och Wiksell, 1927).

——, *The Political Element in the Development of Economic Theory*, translated from the German by P. Streeten (London: Routledge and Kegan Paul, 1953), originally published in Swedish under the title *Vetenskap och politik i nationalekonomien* (Stockholm: Norstedt, 1930); a German translation by Gerhard MacKenroth was entitled *Das politische Element in der nationalökonomischen Doktrinbildung* (Berlin: Junker und Dunnhaupt, 1932); the English translation reappeared in 1990 with a new introduction by R. Swedberg (New Brunswick, NJ: Transaction Publishers, 1990).

——, *The Cost of Living in Sweden* (London: P. S. King and Son, 1933).

——, *Monetary Equilibrium*, English translation by B. B. Bryce and N. Stolper (London: William Hodge and Co., 1939); the initial statement of this line of analysis appeared in Swedish in a 1931 issue of *Ekonomisk tidskrift* under the title 'Om penningteoretisk jämvikt'; a slightly amended version appeared in German entitled 'Der Gleichgewichtsberiff als Instrument der Geldtheoretischen Analyse,' in *Beträge zur Geldtheorie*, F. A. Hayek, ed. (Vienna, 1933), translated by Gerhard Mackenroth.

——, *Konjunktur och offentlig hushållning* (Business Cycles and Public Finance), Appendix III to the Budget Message presented to the Swedish Parliament, January 1933.

——, *Finanspolitikens ekonomiska verkningar* (The Economic Effects of Fiscal Policy), prepared for the Swedish government, 1934.

—— (with Alva Myrdal), *Kris i befolkningsfrågan* (Crisis in the Population Question), (Stockholm: Bonnier, 1934).

——, *Population: A Problem for Democracy* (Cambridge, MA: Harvard University Press, 1940).

—— (with Alva Myrdal), *Kontakt med Amerika* (Contact with America), (Stockholm: Bonnier, 1941).

——, *An American Dilemma: The Negro Problem and American Democracy* (New York: Harper and Brothers, 1944).

——, *Varning för fredsoptimism* (Warning for Peace Optimism), (Stockholm: Bonnier, 1944).

——, *An International Economy: Problems and Prospects* (New York: Harper and Brothers, 1956).

——, *Development and Underdevelopment: A Note on the Mechanism of National and International Economic Inequality* (Cairo: National Bank of Egypt Fiftieth Anniversary Commemoration Lectures, 1956).
——, *Economic Theory and Underdeveloped Regions* (London: Duckworth, 1957); the American edition was entitled *Rich Lands and Poor* (New York: Harper and Brothers, 1957).
——, *Asian Drama: An Inquiry into the Poverty of Nations* (New York: Twentieth Century Fund, 1968).
——, *Challenge to Affluence* (New York: Pantheon Books, 1963).
——, *The Challenge of World Poverty: A World Anti-Poverty Program in Outline* (New York: Pantheon Books, 1970).
——, *Value in Social Theory*, P. Streeten, ed. (London: Routledge and Kegan Paul, 1958).
——, *Against the Stream* (New York: Pantheon Books, 1973).

Articles and other contributions (in the order discussed in the text)

Myrdal, G., 'Gustav Cassel in Memoriam (1866–1944),' English translation by G. Ohlin in *Oxford Institute of Economics and Statistics Bulletin*, 25 (February 1963); this obituary originally appeared in Swedish in *Ekonomisk revy*, 2 (February 1945).
——, 'Industrialization and Population,' *Economic Essays in Honour of Gustav Cassel* (London: George Allen and Unwin, Ltd, 1933).
——, 'Socialpolitikens dilemma' (The Dilemma of Social Policy), *Spektrum* 2:4 (1932).
——, 'Fiscal Policy in the Business Cycle,' *American Economic Review Supplement*, 29 (March 1939).
——, 'Population Problems and Policies,' *Annals of the American Academy of Political and Social Science*, 197 (May 1938).
——, 'Therapy to Heal America's Wounded Psyche,' *Today's Health*, 51 (August 1973).
——, 'Liberalism and the Negro: a Round-Table Discussion,' *Commentary* (March 1964).
——, 'A Worried America,' *Christian Century* (14 December 1977).
——, 'Is American Business Deluding Itself?,' *Atlantic Monthly*, 174 (November 1974).
——, 'The Reconstruction of World Trade and Swedish Trade Policy'; English translation of a paper read to the Swedish National Economic Society, Stockholm, December 1946.
——, 'The Research Work of the Secretariat of the Economic Commission for Europe,' *25 Economic Essays in Honour of Erik Lindahl* (Stockholm: *Ekonomisk tidskrift*, 1956).
——, 'Prospects of the Economic Commission for Europe,' *United Nations Weekly Bulletin*, 3 (29 July 1947).
——, 'Twenty Years of the United Nations Economic Commission for Europe,' *International Organization*, 22 (1968).

——, 'The Trend Towards Economic Planning,' *The Manchester School*, 19 (January 1951).
——, 'Psychological Impediments to Effective International Cooperation,' *Journal of Social Issues*, Supplemental Series 6 (1952).
——, 'Realities and Illusions in Regard to Inter-governmental Organizations,' L. T. Hobhouse Memorial lecture, Bedford College, London (London: Oxford University Press, 1955).
——, 'International Inequality and Foreign Aid in Retrospect,' *Pioneers in Development*, G. M. Meier and D. Seers, eds (New York: Oxford University Press, published for the World Bank, 1984).
——, 'Getting America Moving,' *New Republic*, 184 (26 January 1963).
——, 'Are the Developing Countries Really Developing?,' *Bulletin of the Atomic Scientists*, 27 (January 1971).

Other works

Angresano, J., *The Political Economy of Gunnar Myrdal* (Cheltenham, UK: Edward Elgar, 1997).
Aptheker, H., *The Negro People in America: A Critique of Gunnar Myrdal's An American Dilemma* (New York: International Publishers, 1946).
Appelqvist, Ö. and S. Andersson, *The Essential Gunnar Myrdal* (New York and London: The New Press, 2005).
Balogh, T., 'The Scrutable East,' *New York Times Book Review* (24 March 1968).
Barber, W. J., *British Economic Thought and India, 1600–1858* (Oxford: Clarendon Press, 1975).
——, 'The Kennedy Years: Purposeful Pedagogy,' *Exhortation and Controls: The Search for a Wage-Price Policy, 1945–1971*, C. D. Goodwin, ed. (Washington, DC: The Brookings Institution, 1975).
——, *From New Era to New Deal: Herbert Hoover, the Economists, and American Economic Policy, 1921–1933* (New York and Cambridge: Cambridge University Press, 1985).
——, 'The Career of Alvin Hansen in the 1920s and 1930s: a Study in Intellectual Transformation,' *History of Political Economy*, 19 (Summer 1987).
Bauer, P. T., 'Million-word Pamphlet,' *Spectator*, 222 (10 January 1969).
Blaug, M., *Economic Theory in Retrospect*, 2nd edition (Cambridge: Cambridge University Press, 1968) and 3rd edition (1978).
Bok, S., *Alva Myrdal: A Daughter's Memoir* (Reading, MA: Addison Wesley Publishing Co., 1991).
Boulding, K., 'Warning to Nineveh,' *The Christian Century*, 73:Pt 2 (12 September 1956).
——, 'Asia: Soft States and Hard Facts,' *New Republic*, 157 (4 May 1968).
Bunche, R., *The Political Status of the Negro in the Age of FDR* (Chicago: University of Chicago Press, 1973).
Cassel, G., *The Theory of Social Economy*, new and revised edition (New York: Harcourt Brace and Co., 1932).

Craven, E., 'Gösta Bagge, the Rockefeller Foundation and Empirical Social Science Research in Sweden, 1924–1940,' *The Stockholm School of Economics Revisited*, L. Jonung, ed. (Cambridge and New York: Cambridge University Press, 1991).

Dave, R., *Commerce* (29 July 1968).

DuBois, W. E. B., 'The American Dilemma,' *Phylon: The Atlanta University Review of Race and Culture*, 5 (Second Quarter 1944).

Duesenberry, J., *Income, Savings, and the Theory of Consumer Behavior* (Cambridge, MA: Harvard University Press, 1949).

Eastland, J. O., 'An Alien Ideology Is Not the Law of Our Republic,' *The American Mercury* (March 1958).

Ellis, H., 'Review of Myrdal's *Monetary Equilibrium*,' *Journal of Political Economy*, 48 (June 1940).

Ellison, R., *Shadow and Act* (New York: Random House, 1964).

Fischer, J., 'Western Intellectuals vs. Myrdal's Brutal Facts,' *Harper's Magazine* (June 1968).

Fisher, I., *The Works of Irving Fisher: A Crusader for Social Causes*, Vol. 13, W. J. Barber, ed. (London: Pickering and Chatto, 1997).

Geertz, C., 'Myrdal's Methodology: "Modernism" and the Third World,' *Encounter*, XXXIII (July 1969).

Girod, R., 'How the Public Is Told About the Results of Surveys Carried Out by International Organizations,' *UNESCO: International Social Science Bulletin*, 4:4 (1952).

Girson, R., 'Mutations in the Body Politic,' *Saturday Review* (29 August 1964).

Gupta, K. P., 'Review of *Asian Drama*,' *Commonwealth*, LXXXIX (4 October 1968).

Gustafsson, B., 'A Perennial of Doctrinal History,' *Economy and History*, XVI (1973).

Handlin, O., 'A Book that Changed American Life,' *New York Times Book Review* (21 April 1963).

Hansen, A. H., 'Economic Progress and Declining Population Growth,' *American Economic Review*, 29 (March 1939).

——, 'Mr. Keynes on Underemployment Equilibrium,' *American Economic Review*, 29 (March 1939).

Hansson, B. A., *The Stockholm School and the Development of Dynamic Method* (London: Croom Helm, 1982).

Henriksson, R. G. H., 'The Political Economy Club,' L. Jonung, ed., *The Stockholm School of Economics Revisited* (Cambridge and New York: Cambridge University Press, 1991).

Herskovits, M. J., *The Myth of the Negro Past* (New York and London: Harper and Brothers, 1941).

Hicks, J., Review of 'The Political Element in the Development of Economic Theory,' *Economic Journal*, 64 (December 1954).

——, *Money, Interest and Wages: Collected Essays on Economic Theory*, II (Cambridge, MA: Harvard University Press, 1982).

Jackson, W. A., *Gunnar Myrdal and America's Conscience: Social Engineering and Racial Liberalism, 1938–1987* (Chapel Hill: University of North Carolina Press, 1990).

Johnson, C. S., *Patterns of Negro Segregation* (New York and London: Harper and Brothers, 1943).

Jonung, L., ed., *The Stockholm School of Economics Revisited* (Cambridge and New York: Cambridge University Press, 1991).

Kahn, R. F., 'The Relation of Home Investment to Unemployment,' *Economic Journal*, 41 (June 1931).

Kaldor, N., 'Recollections of an Economist,' *Banca Nazionale del Lavoro Quarterly Review* (March 1986).

Keynes, J. M., 'The Theory of the Rate of Interest,' *The Lessons of Monetary Experience Essays in Honor of Irving Fisher*, A. D. Gayer, ed. (New York: Farrar and Rhinehart, Inc., 1937).

Lagemann, E. C., *The Politics of Knowledge: The Carnegie Corporation, Philanthropy,and Public Policy* (Middletown, CT: Wesleyan University Press, 1989).

Landgren, K-G., *Den 'nya ekonomien' i Sverige: J. M. Keynes, E. Wigforss, B. Ohlin och utvecklingen, 1927–1939* (The 'New Economics' in Sweden: J. M. Keynes, E. Wigforss, B. Ohlin and Developments, 1927–1939), (Stockholm: Almquist och Wiksell, 1960).

Lerner, A. P., 'Some Swedish Stepping Stones in Economic Theory,' *Canadian Journal of Economics and Political Science*, 6 (November 1940).

Lindahl, E., Review of *'Dynamic Pricing,' Economic Journal*, 39 (March 1929).

Lundberg, E., *Business Cycles and Economic Policy* (London: George Allen and Unwin, 1957).

Machlup, F., 'Review of *The Political Element in the Development of Economic Theory*,' *American Economic Review*, 45 (December 1955).

Mahalanobis, P. C., 'The Asian Drama: an Indian View,' *Economic and Political Weekly* (Bombay, July 1969).

Makower, H., 'Review of *An International Economy*,' *American Economic Review*, 46 (December 1956).

Mason, E. S., 'Review of *Das politische Element in der nationalökonomischen Doktrinbildung*,' *Journal of Political Economy*, 42 (April 1934).

Mill, J., *The History of British India* (London: Baldwin, Cradock, and Joy, 1817).

Möller, G., 'The Unemployment Policy,' *Annals of the American Academy of Political and Social Science*, 197 (May 1938).

Myint, H., 'Review of *Asian Drama*,' *Swedish Journal of Economics*, 70 (1968).

Myrdal, A., 'A Program for Family Security in Sweden,' *International Labour Review*, 39 (June 1939).

Ohlin, B., 'Some Notes on the Stockholm Theory of Savings and Investment-I,' *Economic Journal*, 47 (March 1937).

——, 'Some Notes on the Stockholm Theory of Savings and Investment-II,' *Economic Journal*, 47 (June 1937).

——, 'Some Comments on Keynesianism and the Swedish School before 1935,' D. Patinkin and J. C. Leith, eds, *Keynes, Cambridge, and the General Theory* (London: Macmillan, 1977).

——, 'Economic Recovery and Labour Market Problems in Sweden: I,' *International Labour Review*, XXXI (April 1935).

Palander, T., 'On the Concepts and Methods of the "Stockholm School",' *International Economic Papers*, 3 (London and New York: Macmillan, 1953).
Papanek, G. F., 'Review of *Asian Drama*,' *The American Journal of Sociology*, 74 (July 1968).
Patinkin, D., 'Some Observations on Ohlin's 1933 Article,' *History of Political Economy*, 10 (Fall 1978).
—— and J. C. Leith, eds, *Keynes, Cambridge, and the General Theory* (London: Macmillan, 1977).
Rosen, G., 'Review of *Asian Drama*,' *American Economic Review*, LVIII (December 1968).
Rostow, W. W., 'The Economic Commission for Europe,' *International Organization*, 3 (May 1949).
—— and E. Rostow, 'Mr. Myrdal Brings Utilitarianism Up to Date,' *The Reporter*, 15 (12 July 1956).
Samuelson, P., 'Review of Myrdal's *Monetary Equilibrium*,' *American Economic Review*, 30 (March 1940).
Sandelin, B., ed., *Swedish Economics*, 2 (London: Routledge, 1998).
Schumpeter, J. A., *History of Economic Analysis* (Oxford: Oxford University Press, 1954).
Shackle, G. L. S., 'Myrdal's Analysis of *Monetary Equilibrium*,' *Oxford Economic Papers*, 7 (March 1945).
——, *The Years of High Theory: Invention and Tradition in Economic Thought* (Cambridge: Cambridge University Press, 1967).
Shehadi, N., 'The LSE and the Stockholm School in the 1930s,' L. Jonung, ed., *The Stockholm School of Economics Revisited* (Cambridge and New York: Cambridge University Press, 1991).
Shukla, S., 'Planning and Educational Development,' *Indian Educational Review*, 5 (July 1970).
Southern, D. W., *Gunnar Myrdal and Black-White Relations: The Use and Abuse of 'An American Dilemma,'* (Baton Rouge and London: Louisiana State University Press, 1987).
Sterner, R., *The Negro's Share* (New York and London: Harper and Brothers, 1943).
Streeten, P., 'Recent Controversies,' *The Political Element in the Development of Economic Theory* (London: Routledge and Kegan Paul, 1953).
——, 'Economic Models and Their Usefulness for Planning in South Asia,' Appendix 3, *Asian Drama: An Inquiry Into the Poverty of Nations* (New York: Twentieth Century Fund, 1968).
—— and A. Malik, 'Asian Drama Revisited,' *The South Asian Challenge*, K. Haq, ed. (Bangalore: Oxford University Press, 2002).
Steiger, O., 'Bertil Ohlin and the Origins of the Keynesian Revolution,' *History of Political Economy*, 8 (Fall 1976).
Swedberg, R., 'Introduction to the Transaction Edition,' *The Political Element in the Development of Economic Theory* (New Brunswick, NJ: Transaction Publishers, 1990).
Thapur, R., 'Poverty of Nations or Notions,' *Yojana* (12 May 1968).
Thirlwall, A. P., *Nicholas Kaldor* (New York: New York University Press, 1987).

Thomas, B., *Monetary Policy and Crises: A Study of Swedish Experience* (London: George Routledge and Sons, 1936).
Uhr, C. G., 'Economists and Policymaking 1930–1936: Sweden's Experience,' *History of Political Economy*, 9 (Spring 1977).
——, 'The Emergence of the "New Economics" in Sweden: a Review of a Study by Otto Steiger,' *History of Political Economy*, 5 (Spring 1973).
Urquhart, B., *Ralph Bunche: An American Life* (New York and London: W. W. Norton and Co., 1993).
Veblen, T., 'Why Is Economics Not an Evolutionary Science?,' *Quarterly Journal of Economics*, 12 (July 1898).
Velupillai, K., 'Reflections on Gunnar Myrdal's Contributions to Economic Theory,' G. Dostaler, D. Ethier, L. Lepage, eds, *Gunnar Myrdal and His Works* (Montreal: Harvest House, 1992).
Von Mises, L., 'Myrdal's Economics,' *The Freeman* (5 April 1954).
Wadensjö, E., 'The Committee on Unemployment and the Stockholm School,' L. Jonung, ed., *The Stockholm School of Economics Revisited* (Cambridge and New York: Cambridge University Press, 1991).
Wagle, S. S., 'An Inquiry into the Poverty of Nations,' *United Asia* 20 (August 1968).
Wicksell, K., 'Professor Cassel's System of Economics,' reproduced in B. Sandelin, ed., *Swedish Economics*, 2 (London: Routledge, 1998).
Wigforss, E., 'The Financial Policy During Depression and Boom,' *Annals of the American Academy of Political and Social Science*, 197 (May 1938).
Wightman, D., *Economic Cooperation in Europe: A Study of the United Nations Economic Commission for Europe* (London: Stevens and Sons Ltd and William Heineman Ltd, 1956).
Wilkerson, D. A., 'Introduction' to H. Aptheker, *The Negro People in America: A Critique of Gunnar Myrdal's 'An American Dilemma'* (New York: International Publishers, 1946).
Winch, D., 'The Keynesian Revolution in Sweden,' *Journal of Political Economy*, 74 (February 1966).

Index

Made in the USA
Monee, IL
13 September 2026

62976827R00108